KV-373-636

YOUR PERSONAL
HOROSCOPE
2008

LIBRA

YOUR PERSONAL
HOROSCOPE
2008

LIBRA

24th September–23rd October

igloo

This edition published by Igloo Books Ltd,
Cottage Farm, Mears Ashby Road, Sywell, Northants NN6 0BJ
www.igloo-books.com
E-mail: Info@igloo-books.com

Produced for Igloo Books by W. Foulsham & Co. Ltd,
The Publishing House, Bennetts Close, Cippenham,
Slough, Berkshire SL1 5AP, England

ISBN: 978-1-845-61612-0

This is an abridged version of material
originally published in *Old Moore's Horoscope
and Astral Diary*.

Printed in China

CONTENTS

INTRODUCTION

Your Personal Horoscopes have been specifically created to allow you to get the most from astrological patterns and the way they have a bearing on not only your zodiac sign, but nuances within it. Using the diary section of the book you can read about the influences and possibilities of each and every day of the year. It will be possible for you to see when you are likely to be cheerful and happy or those times when your nature is in retreat and you will be more circumspect. The diary will help to give you a feel for the specific 'cycles' of astrology and the way they can subtly change your day-to-day life. For example, when you see the sign ☿, this means that the planet Mercury is retrograde at that time. Retrograde means it appears to be running backwards through the zodiac. Such a happening has a significant effect on communication skills, but this is only one small aspect of how the Personal Horoscope can help you.

With Your Personal Horoscope the story doesn't end with the diary pages. It includes simple ways for you to work out the zodiac sign the Moon occupied at the time of your birth, and what this means for your personality. In addition, if you know the time of day you were born, it is possible to discover your Ascendant, yet another important guide to your personal make-up and potential.

Many readers are interested in relationships and in knowing how well they get on with people of other astrological signs. You might also be interested in the way you appear to very different sorts of individuals. If you are such a person, the section on Venus will be of particular interest. Despite the rapidly changing position of this planet, you can work out your Venus sign, and learn what bearing it will have on your life.

Using Your Personal Horoscope you can travel on one of the most fascinating and rewarding journeys that anyone can take – the journey to a better realisation of self.

THE ESSENCE OF LIBRA

Exploring the Personality of Libra the Scales

(24TH SEPTEMBER – 23RD OCTOBER)

What's in a sign?

At heart you may be the least complicated of all the zodiac sign types, though your ruling element is Air, and that is always going to supply some surprises. Diplomatic, kind and affectionate, your nature blows like a refreshing breeze through the lives of almost anyone you meet. It isn't like you to be gloomy for very long at a time, and you know how to influence the world around you.

It's true that you don't like dirt, or too much disorganisation, and you tend to be very artistic by inclination. You get your own way in life, not by dint of making yourself unpopular in any way but rather with the sort of gentle persuasion to which almost everyone you know falls victim at one time or another. Being considerate of others is more or less second nature to you, though you may not be quite as self-sacrificing as sometimes appears to be the case. You definitely know what you want from life and are not above using a little subterfuge when it comes to getting it.

You are capable and resourceful, but just a little timid on occasions. All the same, when dealing with subject matter that you know and relish, few can better you out there in the practical world. You know how to order your life and can be just as successful in a career sense as you tend to be in your home life. There are times when personal attractions can be something of a stumbling block because you love readily and are very influenced by the kindness and compliments of those around you.

Librans do need to plan ahead, but don't worry about this fact too much because you are also extremely good at thinking on your feet. Getting others to do your bidding is a piece of cake because you are not tardy when it comes to showing your affections. Nevertheless you need to be careful not to allow yourself to fall into unreliable company, or to get involved in schemes that seem too good to be true – some of them are. But for most of the time you present a happy picture to the world and get along just fine, with your ready smile and adaptable personality. You leave almost any situation happier and more contented than it was when you arrived.

Libra resources

When it comes to getting on in life you have as much ammunition in your armoury as most zodiac signs and a great deal more than some. For starters you are adaptable and very resourceful. When you have to take a leap in logic there is nothing preventing you from doing so, and the strong intuition of which your zodiac sign is capable can prove to be very useful at times.

One of your strongest points is the way you manage to make others love you. Although you might consider yourself to be distinctly 'ordinary', that's not the way the world at large perceives you. Most Librans have the ability to etch themselves onto the minds of practically everyone they come across. Why? It's simple. You listen to what people have to say and appear to be deeply interested. On most occasions you are, but even if the tale is a tedious one you give the impression of being rooted to the spot with a determination to hear the story right through. When it comes to responding you are extremely diplomatic and always manage to steer a sensible course between any two or more opposing factions.

Having said that you don't like dirt or untidy places, this is another fact that you can turn to your advantage, because you can always find someone who will help you out. So charming can Libra be that those who do all they can to make you more comfortable regularly end up feeling that you have done them a favour.

It is the sheer magic of the understated Libran that does the trick every time. Even on those rare occasions when you go out with all guns blazing to get what you want from life, you are very unlikely to make enemies on the way. Of course you do have to be careful on occasions, like everyone, but you can certainly push issues further than most. Why? Mainly because people don't realise that you are doing so.

You could easily sell any commodity – though it might be necessary to believe in it yourself first. Since you can always see the good points in anything and tend to be generally optimistic, that should not be too problematical either.

Beneath the surface

In many respects Libra could be the least complicated sign of the zodiac so it might be assumed that 'what you see is what you get'. Life is rarely quite that simple, though you are one of the most straightforward people when it comes to inner struggle. The fact is that most Librans simply don't have a great deal. Between subconscious motivation and in-your-face action there is a seamless process. Librans do need to be loved and this fact can be quite a strong motivation in itself towards any particular course of action. However, even this desire for affection isn't the most powerful factor when considering the sign of the Scales.

What matters most to you is balance, which is probably not at all surprising considering what your zodiac sign actually means. Because of this you would go to tremendous lengths to make sure that your inner resolves create the right external signs and actions to offer the peace that you are looking for most of all.

Like most people born under the Air signs you are not quite as confident as you sometimes appear to be. In the main you are modest and not given to boasting, so you don't attract quite the level of attention of your fellow Air signs, Gemini and Aquarius. All the same you are quite capable of putting on an act when it's necessary to give a good account of yourself in public. You could be quaking inside but you do have the ability to hide this from the world at large.

Librans exhibit such a strong desire to be kind to everyone they meet that they may hide their inner feelings from some people altogether. It's important to remember to be basically honest, even if that means upsetting others a little. This is the most difficult trait for Libra to deal with and may go part of the way to explaining why so many relationship break-ups occur for people born under this zodiac sign. However, as long as you find ways and means to explain your deepest emotional needs, at least to those you love, all should be well.

In most respects you tend to be an open book, particularly to those who take the trouble to look. Your nature is not over-deep, and you are almost certainly not on some secret search to find the 'real you'. Although Libra is sometimes accused of being superficial there are many people in the world who would prefer simplicity to complications and duplicity.

Making the best of yourself

This may be the easiest category by far for the zodiac sign of Libra. The fact is that you rarely do anything else but offer the best version of what you are. Presentation is second nature to Libra, which just loves to be noticed. Despite this you are naturally modest and so not inclined to go over the top in company. You can be relied upon to say and do the right things for most of the time. Even when you consider your actions to be zany and perhaps less acceptable, this is not going to be the impression that the majority of people would get.

In a work sense you need to be involved in some sort of occupation that is clean, allows for a sense of order and ultimately offers the ability to use your head as well as your hands. The fact is that you don't care too much for unsavoury sorts of work and need to be in an environment that suits your basically refined nature. If the circumstances are right you can give a great deal to your work and will go far. Librans also need to be involved with others because they are natural co-operators. For this reason you may not be at your best when working alone or in situations that necessitate all the responsibilities being exclusively yours.

When in the social mainstream you tend to make the best of yourself by simply being what you naturally are. You don't need frills and fancies. Libra is able to make the best sort of impression by using the natural qualities inherent in the sign. As a result, your natural poise, your ability to cut through social divisions, your intelligence and your adaptability should all ensure that you remain popular.

What may occasionally prove difficult is being quite as dominant as the world assumes you ought to be. Many people equate efficiency with power. This is not the way of people born under the Scales, and you need to make that fact plain to anyone who seems to have the desire to shape you.

The impressions you give

Although the adage 'what you see is what you get' may be truer for Libra than for any of its companion signs, it can't be exclusively the case. However, under almost all circumstances you are likely to make friends. You are a much shrewder operator than sometimes appears to be the case and tend to weigh things in the balance very carefully. Libra can be most things to most people, and that's the sort of adaptability that ensures success at both a social and a professional level.

The chances are that you are already well respected and deeply liked by most of the people you know. This isn't so surprising since you are not inclined to make waves of any sort. Whether or not this leads to you achieving the degree of overall success that you deserve in life is quite a different matter. When impressions count you don't tend to let yourself down, or the people who rely on you. Adapting yourself to suit different circumstances is the meat and drink of your basic nature and you have plenty of poise and charm to disarm even the most awkward of people.

In affairs of the heart you are equally adept at putting others at their ease. There is very little difficulty involved in getting people to show their affection for you and when it comes to romance you are one of the most successful practitioners to be found anywhere. The only slight problem in this area of life, as with others, is that you are so talented at offering people what they want that you might not always be living the sort of life that genuinely suits you. Maybe giving the right impression is a little too important for Libra. A deeper form of honesty from the start would prevent you from having to show a less charming side to your nature in the end.

In most circumstances you can be relied upon to exhibit a warm, affectionate, kind, sincere and interesting face to the world at large. As long as this underpins truthfulness it's hard to understand how Libra could really go far wrong.

The way forward

You must already be fairly confident that you have the necessary skills and natural abilities to get on well in a world that is also filled with other people. From infancy most Librans learn how to rub along with others, whilst offering every indication that they are both adaptable and amenable to change. Your chameleon-like ability to 'change colour' in order to suit prevailing circumstances means that you occasionally drop back to being part of the wallpaper in the estimation of at least some people. A greater ability to make an impression probably would not go amiss sometimes, but making a big fuss isn't your way and you actively seek an uncomplicated sort of life.

Balance is everything to Libra, a fact that means there are times when you end up with nothing at all. What needs to be remembered is that there are occasions when everyone simply has to make a decision. This is the hardest thing in the world for you to do but when you manage it you become even more noticed by the world at large.

There's no doubt that people generally hold you in great affection. They know you to be quite capable and love your easy-going attitude to life. You are rarely judgmental and tend to offer almost anyone the benefit of the doubt. Although you are chatty, and inclined to listen avidly to gossip, it isn't your natural way to be unkind, caustic or backbiting. As a result it would seem that you have all the prerequisites to live an extremely happy life. Alas, things are rarely quite that easy.

It is very important for you to demonstrate to yourself, as well as to others, that you are an individual with thoughts and feelings of your own. So often do you defer to the needs of those around you that the real you gets somewhat squashed on the way. There have to be times when you are willing to say 'yes' or 'no' unequivocally, instead of a noncommittal 'I don't really mind' or 'whatever you think best'. At the end of the day you do have opinions and can lead yourself into the path of some severe frustrations if you are unwilling to voice them in the first place.

Try to be particularly honest in deep, emotional attachments. Many Libran relationships come to grief simply because there isn't enough earthy honesty present in the first place. People knowing how you feel won't make them care for you any less. A fully integrated, truthful Libran, with a willingness to participate in the decision making, turns out to be the person who is both successful and happy.

LIBRA ON THE CUSP

Astrological profiles are altered for those people born at either the beginning or the end of a zodiac sign, or, more properly, on the cusps of a sign. In the case of Libra this would be on the 24th of September and for two or three days after, and similarly at the end of the sign, probably from the 21st to the 23rd of October.

The Virgo Cusp – September 24th to 26th

Here we find a Libran subject with a greater than average sense of responsibility and probably a better potential for success than is usually the case for Libra when taken alone. The Virgoan tendency to take itself rather too seriously is far less likely when the sign is mixed with Libra and the resultant nature is often deeply inspiring, and yet quite centred. The Virgo-cusp Libran has what it takes to break through the red tape of society, and yet can understand the need for its existence in the first place. You are caring and concerned, quick on the uptake and very ready to listen to any point of view but, at the end of the day, you know when it is going to be necessary to take a personal stance and this you are far more willing to do than would be the case for non-cuspid Librans.

Family members are important to you, but you always allow them their own individuality and won't get in the way of their personal need to spread their own wings, even at times when it's hard to take this positive stance. Practically speaking, you are a good home-maker but you also enjoy travelling and can benefit greatly from seeing the way other cultures think and behave. It is true that you can have the single- mindedness of a Virgoan, but even this aspect is modified by the Libran within you, so that you usually try to see alternative points of view and often succeed in doing so.

At work you really come into your own. Not only are you capable enough to deal with just about any eventuality, you are also willing to be flexible and to make up your mind instantly when it proves necessary to do so. Colleagues and subordinates alike tend to trust you. You may consider self-employment, unlike most Librans who are usually very worried by this prospect. Making your way in life is something you tend to take for granted, even when the going gets tough.

What people most like about you is that, despite your tremendously practical approach to life, you can be very zany and retain a sense of fun that is, at its best, second to none. Few people find you difficult to understand or to get on with in a day-to-day sense.

The Scorpio Cusp – October 21st to 23rd

The main difference between this cusp and the one at the Virgo end of Libra, is that you tend to be more emotionally motivated and of a slightly less practical nature. Routines are easy for you to address, though you can become very restless and tend to find your own emotional responses difficult to deal with. Sometimes even you don't understand what makes you tick, and that can be a problem. Actually you are not as complicated as you may have come to believe. It's simply that you have a unique view of life and one that doesn't always match that of the people around you, but as Libra instinctively wants to conform, this can lead to some personal confusion.

In family matters you are responsible, very caring and deeply committed to others. It's probable that you work in some field that finds you in direct contact with the public at large and many Scorpio-cusp Librans choose welfare, social or hospital work as a first choice. When it comes to love, you are flexible in your choice and the necessary attributes to promote a long-lasting and happy relationship are clearly present in your basic nature. If there are problems, they may come about as a result of your inability to choose properly in the first place, because you are the first to offer anyone the benefit of the doubt.

When it comes to the practicalities of life, Scorpio can prove to be extremely useful. It offers an 'edge' to your nature and, as Scorpio is a Fixed sign, you are less likely to lose ground because of lack of confidence than Libra alone would be. Your future can be bright, but only if you are willing to get involved in something that really interests you in the first place. You certainly do not care for getting your hands dirty and tend to gravitate towards more refined positions.

Creative potential is good and you could be very artistic, though if this extends to fine art, at least some of your pictures will have 'dark' overtones that might shock some people, including yourself. At base you are kind, caring, complicated, yet inspiring.

LIBRA AND ITS ASCENDANTS

The nature of every individual on the planet is composed of the rich variety of zodiac signs and planetary positions that were present at the time of their birth. Your Sun sign, which in your case is Libra, is one of the many factors when it comes to assessing the unique person you are. Probably the most important consideration, other than your Sun sign, is to establish the zodiac sign that was rising over the eastern horizon at the time that you were born. This is your Ascending or Rising sign. Most popular astrology fails to take account of the Ascendant, and yet its importance remains with you from the very moment of your birth, through every day of your life. The Ascendant is evident in the way you approach the world, and so, when meeting a person for the first time, it is this astrological influence that you are most likely to notice first. Our Ascending sign essentially represents what we appear to be, while the Sun sign is what we feel inside ourselves.

The Ascendant also has the potential for modifying our overall nature. For example, if you were born at a time of day when Libra was passing over the eastern horizon (this would be around the time of dawn) then you would be classed as a double Libran. As such, you would typify this zodiac sign, both internally and in your dealings with others. However, if your Ascendant sign turned out to be a Water sign, such as Pisces, there would be a profound alteration of nature, away from the expected qualities of Libra.

One of the reasons why popular astrology often ignores the Ascendant is that it has always been rather difficult to establish. We have found a way to make this possible by devising an easy-to-use table, which you will find on page 157 of this book. Using this, you can establish your Ascendant sign at a glance. You will need to know your rough time of birth, then it is simply a case of following the instructions.

For those readers who have no idea of their time of birth it might be worth allowing a good friend, or perhaps your partner, to read through the section that follows this introduction. Someone who deals with you on a regular basis may easily discover your Ascending sign, even though you could have some difficulty establishing it for yourself. A good understanding of this component of your nature is essential if you want to be aware of that 'other person' who is responsible for the way you make contact with the world at large. Your Sun sign, Ascendant sign, and the other pointers in this book will, together, allow you a far better understanding of what makes you tick as an individual. Peeling back the different layers of your astrological make-up can be an enlightening experience, and the Ascendant may represent one of the most important layers of all.

Libra with Libra Ascendant

There is no doubt that you carry the very best of all Libran worlds in your nature, though at the same time there is a definite possibility that you often fall between two stools. The literal advice as a result is that you must sometimes make a decision, even though it isn't all that easy for you to do so. Not everyone understands your easy-going side and there are occasions when you could appear to be too flippant for your own good.

The way you approach the world makes you popular, and there is no doubt at all that you are the most diplomatic person to be found anywhere in the length and breadth of the zodiac. It is your job in life to stop people disagreeing and since you can always see every point of view, you make a good impression on the way.

Relationships can sometimes be awkward for you because you can change your mind so easily. But love is never lacking and you can be fairly certain of a generally happy life. Over-indulging is always a potential problem for Air-sign people such as yourself, and there are times in your life when you must get the rest and relaxation which is so important in funding a strong nervous system. Drink plenty of water to flush out a system that can be over-high in natural salts.

Libra with Scorpio Ascendant

There is some tendency for you to be far more deep than the average Libran would appear to be, and for this reason it is crucial that you lighten up from time to time. Every person with a Scorpio quality needs to remember that there is a happy and carefree side to all events, and your Libran quality should allow you to bear this in mind. Sometimes you try to do too many things at the same time. This is fine if you take the casual overview of Libra, but less sensible when you insist on picking the last bone out of every potential, as is much more the case for Scorpio.

When worries come along, as they sometimes will, be able to listen to what your friends have to say and also realise that they are more than willing to work on your behalf, if only because you are so loyal to them. You do have a quality of self-deception, but this should not get in the way too much if you combine the instinctive actions of Libra with the deep intuition of your Scorpio component.

Probably the most important factor of this combination is your ability to succeed in a financial sense. You make a good manager, but not of the authoritarian sort. Jobs in the media or where you are expected to make up your mind quickly would suit you because there is always an underpinning of practical sense that rarely lets you down.

Libra with Sagittarius Ascendant

A very happy combination this, with a great desire for life in all its forms and a need to push forward the bounds of the possible in a way that few other zodiac sign connections would do. You don't like the unpleasant or ugly in life and yet you are capable of dealing with both if you have to. Giving so much to humanity, you still manage to retain a degree of individuality that would surprise many, charm others, and please all.

On the reverse side of the same coin you might find that you are sometimes accused of being fickle, but this is only an expression of your need for change and variety, which is endemic to both these signs. True, you have more of a temper than would be the case for Libra when taken on its own, but such incidents would see you up and down in a flash, and it is almost impossible for you to bear a grudge of any sort. Routines get on your nerves and you are far happier when you can please yourself and get ahead at your own pace, which is quite fast.

As a lover you can make a big impression and most of you will not go short of affection in the early days, before you choose to commit yourself. Once you do, there is always a chance of romantic problems, but these are less likely when you have chosen carefully in the first place.

Libra with Capricorn Ascendant

It is a fact that Libra is the most patient of the Air signs, though like the others it needs to get things done fairly quickly. Capricorn, on the other hand, will work long and hard to achieve its objectives and will not be thwarted in the end. As a result this is a quite powerful sign combination and one that should lead to ultimate success.

Capricorn is often accused of taking itself too seriously and yet it has an ironic and really very funny sense of humour which only its chief confidants recognise. Libra is lighthearted, always willing to have fun and quite anxious to please. When these two basic types come together in their best forms, you might find yourself to be one of the most well- balanced people around. Certainly you know what you want, but you don't have to use a bulldozer in order to get it.

Active and enthusiastic when something really takes your fancy, you might also turn out to be one of the very best lovers of them all. The reason for this is that you have the depth of Capricorn but the lighter and more directly affectionate qualities of the Scales. What you want from life in a personal sense, you eventually tend to get, but you don't care too much if this takes you a while. Few people could deny that you are a faithful friend, a happy sort and a deeply magnetic personality.

Libra with Aquarius Ascendant

Stand by for a truly interesting and very inspiring combination here, but one that is sometimes rather difficult to fathom, even for the sort of people who believe themselves to be very perceptive. The reason for this could be that any situation has to be essentially fixed and constant in order to get a handle on it, and this is certainly not the case for the Aquarian–Libran type. The fact is that both these signs are Air signs, and to a certain extent as unpredictable as the wind itself.

To most people you seem to be original, frank, free and very outspoken. Not everything you do makes sense to others, and if you were alive during the hippy era, it is likely that you went around with flowers in your hair, for you are a free-thinking idealist at heart. With age you mature somewhat, but never too much, because you will always see the strange, the comical and the original in life. This is what keeps you young and is one of the factors that makes you so very attractive to members of the opposite sex. Many people will want to 'adopt' you, and you are at your very best when in company.

Much of your effort is expounded on others and yet, unless you discipline yourself a good deal, personal relationships of the romantic sort can bring certain difficulties. Careful planning is necessary.

Libra with Pisces Ascendant

An Air and Water combination, you are not easy to understand and have depths that show at times, surprising those people who thought they already knew what you were. You will always keep people guessing and are just as likely to hitchhike around Europe as you are to hold down a steady job, both of which you would undertake with the same degree of commitment and success. Usually young at heart, but always carrying the potential for an old head on young shoulders, you are something of a paradox and not at all easy for totally 'straight' types to understand. But you always make an impression and tend to be very attractive to members of the opposite sex.

In matters of health you do have to be a little careful because you dissipate much nervous energy and can sometimes be inclined to push yourself too hard, at least in a mental sense. Frequent periods of rest and meditation will do you the world of good and should improve your level of wisdom, which tends to be fairly high already. Much of your effort in life is expounded on behalf of humanity as a whole, for you care deeply, love totally and always give of your best. Whatever your faults and failings might be, you are one of the most popular people around.

Libra with Aries Ascendant

Libra has the tendency to bring out the best in any zodiac sign, and this is no exception when it comes together with Aries. You may, in fact, be the most comfortable of all Aries types, simply because Libra tempers some of your more assertive qualities and gives you the chance to balance out opposing forces, both inside yourself and in the world outside. You are fun to be with and make the staunchest friend possible. Although you are generally affable, few people would try to put one over on you because they would quickly come to know how far you are willing to go before you let forth a string of invective that would shock those who previously underestimated your basic Aries traits.

Home and family are very dear to you, but you are more tolerant than some Aries types are inclined to be and you have a youthful zest for life that should stay with you no matter what age you manage to achieve. There is always something interesting to do and your mind is a constant stream of possibilities. This makes you very creative and you may also demonstrate a desire to look good at all times. You may not always be quite as confident as you appear to be, but few would guess the fact.

Libra with Taurus Ascendant

A fortunate combination in many ways, this is a double-Venus rulership, since both Taurus and Libra are heavily reliant on the planet of love. You are social, amiable and a natural diplomat, anxious to please and ready to care for just about anyone who shows interest in you. You hate disorder, which means that there is a place for everything and everything in its place. This can throw up the odd paradox however, since being half Libran you cannot always work out where that place ought to be! You deal with life in a humorous way and are quite capable of seeing the absurd in yourself, as well as in others. Your heart is no bigger than that of the quite typical Taurean, but it sits rather closer to the surface and so others recognise it more.

On those occasions when you know you are standing on firm ground you can show great confidence, even if you have to be ready to change some of your opinions at the drop of a hat. When this happens you can be quite at odds with yourself, because Taurus doesn't take very many U-turns, whereas Libra does. Don't expect to know yourself too well, and keep looking for the funny side of things, because it is within humour that you forge the sort of life that suits you best.

Libra with Gemini Ascendant

What a happy-go-lucky soul you are and how popular you tend to be with those around you. Libra is, like Gemini, an Air sign and this means that you are the communicator par excellence, even by Gemini standards. It can sometimes be difficult for you to make up your mind about things because Libra does not exactly aid this process, and especially not when it is allied to Mercurial Gemini. Frequent periods of deep thought are necessary, and meditation would do you a great deal of good. All the same, although you might sometimes be rather unsure of yourself, you are rarely without a certain balance. Clean and tidy surroundings suit you the best, though this is far from easy to achieve because you are invariably dashing off to some place or other, so you really need someone to sort things out in your absence.

The most important fact of all is that you are much loved by your friends, of which there are likely to be very many. Because you are so willing to help them out, in return they are usually there when it matters and they would probably go to almost any length on your behalf. You exhibit a fine sense of justice and will usually back those in trouble. Charities tend to be attractive to you and you do much on behalf of those who live on the fringes of society or people who are truly alone.

Libra with Cancer Ascendant

What an absolutely pleasant and approachable sort of person you are, and how much you have to offer. Like most people associated with the sign of Cancer you give yourself freely to the world, and will always be on hand if anyone is in trouble or needs the special touch you can bring to almost any problem. Behaving in this way is the biggest part of what you are and so people come to rely on you very heavily. Like Libra you can see both sides of any coin and you exhibit the Libran tendency to jump about from one foot to the other when it is necessary to make decisions relating to your own life. This is not usually the case when you are dealing with others however, because the cooler and more detached qualities of Cancer will show through in these circumstances.

It would be fair to say that you do not deal with routines as well as Cancer alone might do and you need a degree of variety in your life, which in your case often comes in the form of travel, which can be distant and of long duration. It isn't unusual for people who have this zodiac combination to end up living abroad, though even this does little to prevent you from getting itchy feet from time to time. In romance you show an original quality that keeps the relationship young and working very well.

Libra with Leo Ascendant

Libra brings slightly more flexibility to the fixed quality of the Leo nature. On the whole you do not represent a picture that is so much different from other versions of the Lion, though you find more time to smile, enjoy changing your mind a great deal more and have a greater number of casual friends. Few would find you proud or haughty and you retain the common touch that can be so important when it comes to getting on in life generally. At work you like to do something that brings variety, and would probably soon tire of doing the same task over and over again. Many of you are teachers, for you have patience, allied to a stubborn core. This can be an indispensable combination on occasions and is part of the reason for the material success that many folk with this combination of signs achieve.

It isn't often that you get down in the dumps, after all there is generally something more important around the next corner, and you love the cut and thrust of everyday life. You always manage to stay young at heart, no matter what your age might be, and you revel in the company of interesting and stimulating types. Maybe you should try harder to concentrate on one thing at once and also strive to retain a serious opinion for more than ten minutes at a time. However, Leo helps to control your flighty tendencies.

Libra with Virgo Ascendant

Libra has the ability to lighten almost any load, and it is particularly good at doing so when it is brought together with the much more repressed sign of Virgo. To the world at large you seem relaxed, happy and able to cope with most of the pressures that life places upon you. Not only do you deal with your own life in a bright and breezy manner but you are usually on hand to help others out of any dilemma that they might make for themselves. With excellent powers of communication, you leave the world at large in no doubt whatsoever concerning both your opinions and your wishes. It is in the talking stakes that you really excel because Virgo brings the silver tongue of Mercury and Libra adds the Air-sign desire to be in constant touch with the world outside your door.

You like to have a good time and can often be found in the company of interesting and stimulating people, who have the ability to bring out the very best in your bright and sparkling personality. Underneath however, there is still much of the worrying Virgoan to be found and this means that you have to learn to relax inside as well as appearing to do so externally. In fact you are much more complex than most people would realise, and definitely would not be suited to a life that allowed you too much time to think about yourself.

THE MOON AND THE PART IT PLAYS IN YOUR LIFE

In astrology the Moon is probably the single most important heavenly body after the Sun. Its unique position, as partner to the Earth on its journey around the solar system, means that the Moon appears to pass through the signs of the zodiac extremely quickly. The zodiac position of the Moon at the time of your birth plays a great part in personal character and is especially significant in the build-up of your emotional nature.

Your Own Moon Sign

Discovering the position of the Moon at the time of your birth has always been notoriously difficult because tracking the complex zodiac positions of the Moon is not easy. This process has been reduced to three simple stages with our Lunar Tables. A breakdown of the Moon's zodiac positions can be found from page 35 onwards, so that once you know what your Moon Sign is, you can see what part this plays in the overall build-up of your personal character.

If you follow the instructions on the next page you will soon be able to work out exactly what zodiac sign the Moon occupied on the day that you were born and you can then go on to compare the reading for this position with those of your Sun sign and your Ascendant. It is partly the comparison between these three important positions that goes towards making you the unique individual you are.

HOW TO DISCOVER YOUR MOON SIGN

This is a three-stage process. You may need a pen and a piece of paper but if you follow the instructions below the process should only take a minute or so.

STAGE 1 First of all you need to know the Moon Age at the time of your birth. If you look at Moon Table 1, on page 33, you will find all the years between 1910 and 2008 down the left side. Find the year of your birth and then trace across to the right to the month of your birth. Where the two intersect you will find a number. This is the date of the New Moon in the month that you were born. You now need to count forward the number of days between the New Moon and your own birthday. For example, if the New Moon in the month of your birth was shown as being the 6th and you were born on the 20th, your Moon Age Day would be 14. If the New Moon in the month of your birth came after your birthday, you need to count forward from the New Moon in the previous month. If you were born in a Leap Year, remember to count the 29th February. You can tell if your birth year was a Leap Year if the last two digits can be divided by four. Whatever the result, jot this number down so that you do not forget it.

STAGE 2 Take a look at Moon Table 2 on page 34. Down the left hand column look for the date of your birth. Now trace across to the month of your birth. Where the two meet you will find a letter. Copy this letter down alongside your Moon Age Day.

STAGE 3 Moon Table 3 on page 34 will supply you with the zodiac sign the Moon occupied on the day of your birth. Look for your Moon Age Day down the left hand column and then for the letter you found in Stage 2. Where the two converge you will find a zodiac sign and this is the sign occupied by the Moon on the day that you were born.

Your Zodiac Moon Sign Explained

You will find a profile of all zodiac Moon Signs on pages 35 to 38, showing in yet another way how astrology helps to make you into the individual that you are. In each daily entry of the Astral Diary you can find the zodiac position of the Moon for every day of the year. This also allows you to discover your lunar birthdays. Since the Moon passes through all the signs of the zodiac in about a month, you can expect something like twelve lunar birthdays each year. At these times you are likely to be emotionally steady and able to make the sort of decisions that have real, lasting value.

MOON TABLE 1

YEAR	AUG	SEP	OCT	YEAR	AUG	SEP	OCT	YEAR	AUG	SEP	OCT
1910	5	3	2	1943	1/30	29	29	1976	25	23	23
1911	24	22	21	1944	18	17	17	1977	14	13	12
1912	13	12	11	1945	8	6	6	1978	4	2	2/31
1913	2/31	30	29	1946	26	25	24	1979	22	21	20
1914	21	19	19	1947	16	14	14	1980	11	10	9
1915	10	9	8	1948	5	3	2	1981	29	28	27
1916	29	27	27	1949	24	23	21	1982	19	17	17
1917	17	15	15	1950	13	12	11	1983	8	7	6
1918	6	4	4	1951	2	1	1/30	1984	26	25	24
1919	25	23	23	1952	20	19	18	1985	16	14	14
1920	14	12	12	1953	9	8	8	1986	5	4	3
1921	3	2	1/30	1954	28	27	26	1987	24	23	22
1922	22	21	20	1955	17	16	15	1988	12	11	10
1923	12	10	10	1956	6	4	4	1989	1/31	29	29
1924	30	28	28	1957	25	23	23	1990	20	19	18
1925	19	18	17	1958	15	13	12	1991	9	8	8
1926	8	7	6	1959	4	3	2/31	1992	28	26	25
1927	27	25	25	1960	22	21	20	1993	17	16	15
1928	16	14	14	1961	11	10	9	1994	7	5	5
1929	5	3	2	1962	30	28	28	1995	26	24	24
1930	24	22	20	1963	19	17	17	1996	14	13	11
1931	13	12	11	1964	7	6	5	1997	3	2	2/31
1932	2/31	30	29	1965	26	25	24	1998	22	20	20
1933	21	19	19	1966	16	14	14	1999	11	10	8
1934	10	9	8	1967	5	4	3	2000	29	27	27
1935	29	27	27	1968	24	23	22	2001	19	17	17
1936	17	15	15	1969	12	11	10	2002	8	6	6
1937	6	4	4	1970	2	1	1/30	2003	27	26	25
1938	25	23	23	1971	20	19	19	2004	14	13	12
1939	15	13	12	1972	9	8	8	2005	4	3	2
1940	4	2	1/30	1973	28	27	26	2006	23	22	21
1941	22	21	20	1974	17	16	15	2007	13	12	11
1942	12	10	10	1975	7	5	5	2008	1/31	30	29

TABLE 2 MOON TABLE 3

DAY	SEP	OCT	M/D	X	Y	Z	a	b	d	e
1	X	a	0	VI	VI	LI	LI	LI	LI	SC
2	X	a	1	VI	LI	LI	LI	LI	SC	SC
3	X	a	2	LI	LI	LI	LI	SC	SC	SC
4	Y	b	3	LI	LI	SC	SC	SC	SC	SA
5	Y	b	4	LI	SC	SC	SC	SA	SA	SA
6	Y	b	5	SC	SC	SC	SA	SA	SA	CP
7	Y	b	6	SC	SA	SA	SA	CP	CP	CP
8	Y	b	7	SA	SA	SA	SA	CP	CP	AQ
9	Y	b	8	SA	SA	CP	CP	CP	CP	AQ
10	Y	b	9	SA	CP	CP	CP	AQ	AQ	AQ
11	Y	b	10	CP	CP	CP	AQ	AQ	AQ	PI
12	Y	b	11	CP	AQ	AQ	AQ	PI	PI	PI
13	Y	b	12	AQ	AQ	AQ	PI	PI	PI	AR
14	Z	d	13	AQ	AQ	PI	PI	AR	PI	AR
15	Z	d	14	PI	PI	PI	AR	AR	AR	TA
16	Z	d	15	PI	PI	PI	AR	AR	AR	TA
17	Z	d	16	PI	AR	AR	AR	AR	TA	TA
18	Z	d	17	AR	AR	AR	AR	TA	TA	GE
19	Z	d	18	AR	AR	AR	TA	TA	GE	GE
20	Z	d	19	AR	TA	TA	TA	TA	GE	GE
21	Z	d	20	TA	TA	TA	GE	GE	GE	CA
22	Z	d	21	TA	GE	GE	GE	GE	CA	CA
23	Z	d	22	GE	GE	GE	GE	CA	CA	CA
24	a	e	23	GE	GE	GE	CA	CA	CA	LE
25	a	e	24	GE	CA	CA	CA	CA	LE	LE
26	a	e	25	CA	CA	CA	CA	LE	LE	LE
27	a	e	26	CA	LE	LE	LE	LE	VI	VI
28	a	e	27	LE	LE	LE	LE	VI	VI	VI
29	a	e	28	LE	LE	LE	VI	VI	VI	LI
30	a	e	29	LE	VI	VI	VI	VI	LI	LI
31	–	e								

AR = Aries, TA = Taurus, GE = Gemini, CA = Cancer, LE = Leo, VI = Virgo, LI = Libra, SC = Scorpio, SA = Sagittarius, CP = Capricorn, AQ = Aquarius, PI = Pisces

MOON SIGNS

Moon in Aries

You have a strong imagination, courage, determination and a desire to do things in your own way and forge your own path through life.

Originality is a key attribute; you are seldom stuck for ideas although your mind is changeable and you could take the time to focus on individual tasks. Often quick-tempered, you take orders from few people and live life at a fast pace. Avoid health problems by taking regular time out for rest and relaxation.

Emotionally, it is important that you talk to those you are closest to and work out your true feelings. Once you discover that people are there to help, there is less necessity for you to do everything yourself.

Moon in Taurus

The Moon in Taurus gives you a courteous and friendly manner, which means you are likely to have many friends.

The good things in life mean a lot to you, as Taurus is an Earth sign that delights in experiences which please the senses. Hence you are probably a lover of good food and drink, which may in turn mean you need to keep an eye on the bathroom scales, especially as looking good is also important to you.

Emotionally you are fairly stable and you stick by your own standards. Taureans do not respond well to change. Intuition also plays an important part in your life.

Moon in Gemini

You have a warm-hearted character, sympathetic and eager to help others. At times reserved, you can also be articulate and chatty: this is part of the paradox of Gemini, which always brings duplicity to the nature. You are interested in current affairs, have a good intellect, and are good company and likely to have many friends. Most of your friends have a high opinion of you and would be ready to defend you should the need arise. However, this is usually unnecessary, as you are quite capable of defending yourself in any verbal confrontation.

Travel is important to your inquisitive mind and you find intellectual stimulus in mixing with people from different cultures. You also gain much from reading, writing and the arts but you do need plenty of rest and relaxation in order to avoid fatigue.

Moon in Cancer

The Moon in Cancer at the time of birth is a fortunate position as Cancer is the Moon's natural home. This means that the qualities of compassion and understanding given by the Moon are especially enhanced in your nature, and you are friendly and sociable and cope well with emotional pressures. You cherish home and family life, and happily do the domestic tasks. Your surroundings are important to you and you hate squalor and filth. You are likely to have a love of music and poetry.

Your basic character, although at times changeable like the Moon itself, depends on symmetry. You aim to make your surroundings comfortable and harmonious, for yourself and those close to you.

Moon in Leo

The best qualities of the Moon and Leo come together to make you warm-hearted, fair, ambitious and self-confident. With good organisational abilities, you invariably rise to a position of responsibility in your chosen career. This is fortunate as you don't enjoy being an 'also-ran' and would rather be an important part of a small organisation than a menial in a large one.

You should be lucky in love, and happy, provided you put in the effort to make a comfortable home for yourself and those close to you. It is likely that you will have a love of pleasure, sport, music and literature. Life brings you many rewards, most of them as a direct result of your own efforts, although you may be luckier than average and ready to make the best of any situation.

Moon in Virgo

You are endowed with good mental abilities and a keen receptive memory, but you are never ostentatious or pretentious. Naturally quite reserved, you still have many friends, especially of the opposite sex. Marital relationships must be discussed carefully and worked at so that they remain harmonious, as personal attachments can be a problem if you do not give them your full attention.

Talented and persevering, you possess artistic qualities and are a good homemaker. Earning your honours through genuine merit, you work long and hard towards your objectives but show little pride in your achievements. Many short journeys will be undertaken in your life.

Moon in Libra

With the Moon in Libra you are naturally popular and make friends easily. People like you, probably more than you realise, you bring fun to a party and are a natural diplomat. For all its good points, Libra is not the most stable of astrological signs and, as a result, your emotions can be a little unstable too. Therefore, although the Moon in Libra is said to be good for love and marriage, your Sun sign and Rising sign will have an important effect on your emotional and loving qualities.

You must remember to relate to others in your decision-making. Co-operation is crucial because Libra represents the 'balance' of life that can only be achieved through harmonious relationships. Conformity is not easy for you because Libra, an Air sign, likes its independence.

Moon in Scorpio

Some people might call you pushy. In fact, all you really want to do is to live life to the full and protect yourself and your family from the pressures of life. Take care to avoid giving the impression of being sarcastic or impulsive and use your energies wisely and constructively.

You have great courage and you invariably achieve your goals by force of personality and sheer effort. You are fond of mystery and are good at predicting the outcome of situations and events. Travel experiences can be beneficial to you.

You may experience problems if you do not take time to examine your motives in a relationship, and also if you allow jealousy, always a feature of Scorpio, to cloud your judgement.

Moon in Sagittarius

The Moon in Sagittarius helps to make you a generous individual with humanitarian qualities and a kind heart. Restlessness may be intrinsic as your mind is seldom still. Perhaps because of this, you have a need for change that could lead you to several major moves during your adult life. You are not afraid to stand your ground when you know your judgement is right, you speak directly and have good intuition.

At work you are quick, efficient and versatile and so you make an ideal employee. You need work to be intellectually demanding and do not enjoy tedious routines.

In relationships, you anger quickly if faced with stupidity or deception, though you are just as quick to forgive and forget. Emotionally, there are times when your heart rules your head.

Moon in Capricorn

The Moon in Capricorn makes you popular and likely to come into the public eye in some way. The watery Moon is not entirely comfortable in the Earth sign of Capricorn and this may lead to some difficulties in the early years of life. An initial lack of creative ability and indecision must be overcome before the true qualities of patience and perseverance inherent in Capricorn can show through.

You have good administrative ability and are a capable worker, and if you are careful you can accumulate wealth. But you must be cautious and take professional advice in partnerships, as you are open to deception. You may be interested in social or welfare work, which suit your organisational skills and sympathy for others.

Moon in Aquarius

The Moon in Aquarius makes you an active and agreeable person with a friendly, easy-going nature. Sympathetic to the needs of others, you flourish in a laid-back atmosphere. You are broad-minded, fair and open to suggestion, although sometimes you have an unconventional quality which others can find hard to understand.

You are interested in the strange and curious, and in old articles and places. You enjoy trips to these places and gain much from them. Political, scientific and educational work interests you and you might choose a career in science or technology.

Money-wise, you make gains through innovation and concentration and Lunar Aquarians often tackle more than one job at a time. In love you are kind and honest.

Moon in Pisces

You have a kind, sympathetic nature, somewhat retiring at times, but you always take account of others' feelings and help when you can.

Personal relationships may be problematic, but as life goes on you can learn from your experiences and develop a better understanding of yourself and the world around you.

You have a fondness for travel, appreciate beauty and harmony and hate disorder and strife. You may be fond of literature and would make a good writer or speaker yourself. You have a creative imagination and may come across as an incurable romantic. You have strong intuition, maybe bordering on a mediumistic quality, which sets you apart from the mass. You may not be rich in cash terms, but your personal gifts are worth more than gold.

LIBRA IN LOVE

Discover how compatible you are with people from the same and other signs of the zodiac. Five stars equals a match made in heaven!

Libra meets Libra

This is a potentially successful match because Librans are extremely likeable people, and so it stands to reason that two Librans together will be twice as pleasant and twice as much fun. However, Librans can also be indecisive and need an anchor from which to find practical and financial success, and obviously one Libran won't provide this for another. Librans can be flighty in a romantic sense, so both parties will need to develop a steadfast approach for a long-term relationship. Star rating: ****

Libra meets Scorpio

Many astrologers have reservations about this match because, on the surface, the signs are so different. However, this couple may find fulfilment because these differences mean that their respective needs are met. Scorpio needs a partner to lighten the load which won't daunt Libra, while Libra looks for a steadfast quality which it doesn't possess, but Scorpio can supply naturally. Financial success is possible because they both have good ideas and back them up with hard work and determination. All in all, a promising outlook. Star rating: ****

Libra meets Sagittarius

Libra and Sagittarius are both adaptable signs who get on well with most people, but this promising outlook often does not follow through because each brings out the flighty side of the other. This combination is great for a fling, but when the romance is over someone needs to see to the practical side of life. Both signs are well meaning, pleasant and kind, but are either of them constant enough to build a life together? In at least some of the cases, the answer would be no. Star rating: ***

Libra meets Capricorn

Libra and Capricorn rub each other up the wrong way because their attitudes to life are so different, and although both are capable of doing something about this, in reality they probably won't. Capricorn is steady, determined and solid, while Libra is bright but sometimes superficial and not entirely reliable. They usually lack the instant spark needed to get them together in the first place, so when it does happen it is often because one of the partners is not typical of their sign. Star rating: **

Libra meets Aquarius

One of the best combinations imaginable, partly because both are Air signs and so share a common meeting point. But perhaps the more crucial factor is that both signs respect each other. Aquarius loves life and originality, and is quite intellectual. Libra is similar, but more balanced and rather less eccentric. A visit to this couple's house would be entertaining and full of zany wit, activity and excitement. Both are keen to travel and may prefer to 'find themselves' before taking on too many domestic responsibilities. Star rating: *****

Libra meets Pisces

Libra and Pisces can be extremely fond of each other, even deeply in love, but this alone isn't a stable foundation for long-term success. Pisces is extremely deep and doesn't even know itself very well. Libra may initially find this intriguing but will eventually feel frustrated at being unable to understand the Piscean's emotional and personal feelings. Pisces can be jealous and may find Libra's flightiness difficult, which Libra can't stand. They are great friends and they may make it to the romantic stakes, but when they get there a lot of effort will be necessary. Star rating: ***

Libra meets Aries

These are zodiac opposites which means a make-or-break situation. The match will either be a great success or a dismal failure. Why? Well, Aries finds it difficult to understand the flighty Air-sign tendencies of Libra, whilst the natural balance of Libra contradicts the unorthodox Arian methods. Any flexibility will come from Libra, which may mean that things work out for a while, but Libra only has so much patience and it may eventually run out. In the end, Aries may be just too bossy for an independent but sensitive sign like Libra. Star rating: **

Libra meets Taurus

A happy life is important to both these signs and, as they are both ruled by Venus, they share a common understanding, even though they display themselves so differently. Taurus is quieter than Libra, but can be decisive, and that's what counts. Libra is interested in absolutely everything, an infectious quality when seen through Taurean eyes. The slightly flighty qualities of Libra may lead to jealousy from the Bull. Not an argumentative relationship and one that often works well. There could be many changes of address for this pair. Star rating: ****

Libra meets Gemini

One of the best possible zodiac combinations. Libra and Gemini are both Air signs, which leads to a meeting of minds. Both signs simply love to have a good time, although Libra is the tidiest and less forgetful. Gemini's capricious nature won't bother Libra, who acts as a stabilising influence. Life should generally run smoothly, and any rows are likely to be short and sharp. Both parties genuinely like each other, which is of paramount importance in a relationship and, ultimately, there isn't a better reason for being or staying together. Star rating: *****

Libra meets Cancer

Almost anyone can get on with Libra, which is one of the most adaptable signs of them all. But being adaptable does not always lead to fulfilment and a successful match here will require a quiet Libran and a slightly more progressive Cancerian than the norm. Both signs are pleasant and polite, and like domestic order, but Libra may find Cancer too emotional and perhaps lacking in vibrancy, while Libra, on the other hand, may be a little too flighty for steady Cancer. Star rating: ***

Libra meets Leo

The biggest drawback here is likely to be in the issue of commitment. Leo knows everything about constancy and faithfulness, a lesson which, sadly, Libra needs to learn. Librans are easy-going and diplomatic, qualities which are useful when Leo is on the war-path. This couple should be compatible on a personal level and any problems tend to relate to the different way in which these signs deal with outside factors. With good will and an open mind, it can work out well enough. Star rating: ***

Libra meets Virgo

There have been some rare occasions when this match has found great success, but usually the darker and more inward-looking Virgoan depresses the naturally gregarious Libran. Libra appears self-confident, but is not so beneath the surface, and needs encouragement to develop inner confidence, which may not come from Virgo. Constancy can be a problem for Libra, who also tires easily and may find Virgo dull. A lighter, less serious approach to life from Virgo is needed to make this work. Star rating: **

VENUS:
THE PLANET OF LOVE

If you look up at the sky around sunset or sunrise you will often see Venus in close attendance to the Sun. It is arguably one of the most beautiful sights of all and there is little wonder that historically it became associated with the goddess of love. But although Venus does play an important part in the way you view love and in the way others see you romantically, this is only one of the spheres of influence that it enjoys in your overall character.

Venus has a part to play in the more cultured side of your life and has much to do with your appreciation of art, literature, music and general creativity. Even the way you look is responsive to the part of the zodiac that Venus occupied at the start of your life, though this fact is also down to your Sun sign and Ascending sign. If, at the time you were born, Venus occupied one of the more gregarious zodiac signs, you will be more likely to wear your heart on your sleeve, as well as to be more attracted to entertainment, social gatherings and good company. If on the other hand Venus occupied a quiet zodiac sign at the time of your birth, you would tend to be more retiring and less willing to shine in public situations.

It's good to know what part the planet Venus plays in your life for it can have a great bearing on the way you appear to the rest of the world and since we all have to mix with others, you can learn to make the very best of what Venus has to offer you.

One of the great complications in the past has always been trying to establish exactly what zodiac position Venus enjoyed when you were born because the planet is notoriously difficult to track. However, we have solved that problem by creating a table that is exclusive to your Sun sign, which you will find on the following page.

Establishing your Venus sign could not be easier. Just look up the year of your birth on the next page and you will see a sign of the zodiac. This was the sign that Venus occupied in the period covered by your sign in that year. If Venus occupied more than one sign during the period, this is indicated by the date on which the sign changed, and the name of the new sign. For instance, if you were born in 1950, Venus was in Virgo until the 4th October, after which time it was in Libra. If you were born before 4th October your Venus sign is Virgo, if you were born on or after 4th October, your Venus sign is Libra. Once you have established the position of Venus at the time of your birth, you can then look in the pages which follow to see how this has a bearing on your life as a whole.

1910 VIRGO / 6.10 LIBRA	1957 SCORPIO / 10.10 SAGITTARIUS
1911 VIRGO	1958 VIRGO / 4.10 LIBRA
1912 LIBRA / 30.9 SCORPIO	1959 VIRGO / 28.9 LEO
1913 LEO / 27.9 VIRGO /	1960 LIBRA / 27.9 SCORPIO
21.10 LIBRA	1961 VIRGO / 18.10 LIBRA
1914 SCORPIO / 10.10 SAGITTARIUS	1962 SCORPIO / 16.10 SAGITTARIUS
1915 LIBRA / 16.10 SCORPIO	1963 LIBRA / 12.10 SCORPIO
1916 LEO / 8.10 VIRGO	1964 LEO / 6.10 VIRGO
1917 SCORPIO / 12.10 SAGITTARIUS	1965 SCORPIO / 9.10 SAGITTARIUS
1918 VIRGO / 6.10 LIBRA	1966 VIRGO / 4.10 LIBRA
1919 SCORPIO / 12.10 SAGITTARIUS	1967 VIRGO / 3.10 LEO
1920 LIBRA / 30.9 SCORPIO	1968 LIBRA / 26.9 SCORPIO
1921 LEO / 26.9 VIRGO /	1969 VIRGO / 17.10 LIBRA
21.10 LIBRA	1970 SCORPIO / 19.10 SAGITTARIUS
1922 SCORPIO / 11.10 SAGITTARIUS	1971 LIBRA / 11.10 SCORPIO
1923 LIBRA / 16.10 SCORPIO	1972 LEO / 6.10 VIRGO
1924 LEO / 8.10 VIRGO	1973 SCORPIO / 9.10 SAGITTARIUS
1925 SCORPIO / 12.10 SAGITTARIUS	1974 VIRGO / 3.10 LIBRA
1926 VIRGO / 6.10 LIBRA	1975 VIRGO / 5.10 LEO
1927 VIRGO	1976 LIBRA / 26.9 SCORPIO
1928 LIBRA / 29.9 SCORPIO	1977 VIRGO / 17.10 LIBRA
1929 LEO / 26.9 VIRGO /	1978 SCORPIO / 19.10 SAGITTARIUS
20.10 LIBRA	1979 LIBRA / 11.10 SCORPIO
1930 SCORPIO / 12.10 SAGITTARIUS	1980 LEO / 5.10 VIRGO
1931 LIBRA / 15.10 SCORPIO	1981 SCORPIO / 9.10 SAGITTARIUS
1932 LEO / 7.10 VIRGO	1982 VIRGO / 3.10 LIBRA
1933 SCORPIO / 11.10 SAGITTARIUS	1983 VIRGO / 7.10 LEO
1934 VIRGO / 5.10 LIBRA	1984 LIBRA / 25.9 SCORPIO
1935 VIRGO	1985 VIRGO / 16.10 LIBRA
1936 LIBRA / 28.9 SCORPIO	1986 SCORPIO
1937 LEO / 25.9 VIRGO /	1987 LIBRA / 10.10 SCORPIO
20.10 LIBRA	1988 LEO / 5.10 VIRGO
1938 SCORPIO / 14.10 SAGITTARIUS	1989 SCORPIO / 8.10 SAGITTARIUS
1939 LIBRA / 14.10 SCORPIO	1990 VIRGO / 2.10 LIBRA
1940 LEO / 7.10 VIRGO	1991 VIRGO / 8.10 LEO
1941 SCORPIO / 11.10 SAGITTARIUS	1992 LIBRA / 25.9 SCORPIO
1942 VIRGO / 5.10 LIBRA	1993 VIRGO / 16.10 LIBRA
1943 VIRGO	1994 SCORPIO
1944 LIBRA / 28.9 SCORPIO	1995 LIBRA / 10.10 SCORPIO
1945 LEO / 25.9 VIRGO /	1996 LEO / 5.10 VIRGO
19.10 LIBRA	1997 SCORPIO / 8.10 SAGITTARIUS
1946 SCORPIO / 14.10 SAGITTARIUS	1998 VIRGO / 2.10 LIBRA
1947 LIBRA / 13.10 SCORPIO	1999 VIRGO / 9.10 LEO
1948 LEO / 7.10 VIRGO	2000 LIBRA / 25.9 SCORPIO
1949 SCORPIO / 11.10 SAGITTARIUS	2001 LEO / 5.10 VIRGO
1950 VIRGO / 4.10 LIBRA	2002 SCORPIO / 8.10 SAGITTARIUS
1951 VIRGO	2003 LIBRA / 10.10 SCORPIO
1952 LIBRA / 27.9 SCORPIO	2004 LEO / 5.10 VIRGO
1953 VIRGO / 19.10 LIBRA	2005 SCORPIO / 8.10 SAGITTARIUS
1954 SCORPIO / 16.10 SAGITTARIUS	2006 VIRGO / 2.10 LIBRA
1955 LIBRA / 12.10 SCORPIO	2007 VIRGO / 9.10 LEO
1956 LEO / 6.10 VIRGO	2008 LIBRA / 25.9 SCORPIO

VENUS THROUGH THE ZODIAC SIGNS

Venus in Aries

Amongst other things, the position of Venus in Aries indicates a fondness for travel, music and all creative pursuits. Your nature tends to be affectionate and you would try not to create confusion or difficulty for others if it could be avoided. Many people with this planetary position have a great love of the theatre, and mental stimulation is of the greatest importance. Early romantic attachments are common with Venus in Aries, so it is very important to establish a genuine sense of romantic continuity. Early marriage is not recommended, especially if it is based on sympathy. You may give your heart a little too readily on occasions.

Venus in Taurus

You are capable of very deep feelings and your emotions tend to last for a very long time. This makes you a trusting partner and lover, whose constancy is second to none. In life you are precise and careful and always try to do things the right way. Although this means an ordered life, which you are comfortable with, it can also lead you to be rather too fussy for your own good. Despite your pleasant nature, you are very fixed in your opinions and quite able to speak your mind. Others are attracted to you and historical astrologers always quoted this position of Venus as being very fortunate in terms of marriage. However, if you find yourself involved in a failed relationship, it could take you a long time to trust again.

Venus in Gemini

As with all associations related to Gemini, you tend to be quite versatile, anxious for change and intelligent in your dealings with the world at large. You may gain money from more than one source but you are equally good at spending it. There is an inference here that you are a good communicator, via either the written or the spoken word, and you love to be in the company of interesting people. Always on the look-out for culture, you may also be very fond of music, and love to indulge the curious and cultured side of your nature. In romance you tend to have more than one relationship and could find yourself associated with someone who has previously been a friend or even a distant relative.

Venus in Cancer

You often stay close to home because you are very fond of family and enjoy many of your most treasured moments when you are with those you love. Being naturally sympathetic, you will always do anything you can to support those around you, even people you hardly know at all. This charitable side of your nature is your most noticeable trait and is one of the reasons why others are naturally so fond of you. Being receptive and in some cases even psychic, you can see through to the soul of most of those with whom you come into contact. You may not commence too many romantic attachments but when you do give your heart, it tends to be unconditionally.

Venus in Leo

It must become quickly obvious to almost anyone you meet that you are kind, sympathetic and yet determined enough to stand up for anyone or anything that is truly important to you. Bright and sunny, you warm the world with your natural enthusiasm and would rarely do anything to hurt those around you, or at least not intentionally. In romance you are ardent and sincere, though some may find your style just a little overpowering. Gains come through your contacts with other people and this could be especially true with regard to romance, for love and money often come hand in hand for those who were born with Venus in Leo. People claim to understand you, though you are more complex than you seem.

Venus in Virgo

Your nature could well be fairly quiet no matter what your Sun sign might be, though this fact often manifests itself as an inner peace and would not prevent you from being basically sociable. Some delays and even the odd disappointment in love cannot be ruled out with this planetary position, though it's a fact that you will usually find the happiness you look for in the end. Catapulting yourself into romantic entanglements that you know to be rather ill-advised is not sensible, and it would be better to wait before you committed yourself exclusively to any one person. It is the essence of your nature to serve the world at large and through doing so it is possible that you will attract money at some stage in your life.

Venus in Libra

Venus is very comfortable in Libra and bestows upon those people who have this planetary position a particular sort of kindness that is easy to recognise. This is a very good position for all sorts of friendships and also for romantic attachments that usually bring much joy into your life. Few individuals with Venus in Libra would avoid marriage and since you are capable of great depths of love, it is likely that you will find a contented personal life. You like to mix with people of integrity and intelligence but don't take kindly to scruffy surroundings or work that means getting your hands too dirty. Careful speculation, good business dealings and money through marriage all seem fairly likely.

Venus in Scorpio

You are quite open and tend to spend money quite freely, even on those occasions when you don't have very much. Although your intentions are always good, there are times when you get yourself in to the odd scrape and this can be particularly true when it comes to romance, which you may come to late or from a rather unexpected direction. Certainly you have the power to be happy and to make others contented on the way, but you find the odd stumbling block on your journey through life and it could seem that you have to work harder than those around you. As a result of this, you gain a much deeper understanding of the true value of personal happiness than many people ever do, and are likely to achieve true contentment in the end.

Venus in Sagittarius

You are lighthearted, cheerful and always able to see the funny side of any situation. These facts enhance your popularity, which is especially high with members of the opposite sex. You should never have to look too far to find romantic interest in your life, though it is just possible that you might be too willing to commit yourself before you are certain that the person in question is right for you. Part of the problem here extends to other areas of life too. The fact is that you like variety in everything and so can tire of situations that fail to offer it. All the same, if you choose wisely and learn to understand your restless side, then great happiness can be yours.

Venus in Capricorn

The most notable trait that comes from Venus in this position is that it makes you trustworthy and able to take on all sorts of responsibilities in life. People are instinctively fond of you and love you all the more because you are always ready to help those who are in any form of need. Social and business popularity can be yours and there is a magnetic quality to your nature that is particularly attractive in a romantic sense. Anyone who wants a partner for a lover, a spouse and a good friend too would almost certainly look in your direction. Constancy is the hallmark of your nature and unfaithfulness would go right against the grain. You might sometimes be a little too trusting.

Venus in Aquarius

This location of Venus offers a fondness for travel and a desire to try out something new at every possible opportunity. You are extremely easy to get along with and tend to have many friends from varied backgrounds, classes and inclinations. You like to live a distinct sort of life and gain a great deal from moving about, both in a career sense and with regard to your home. It is not out of the question that you could form a romantic attachment to someone who comes from far away or be attracted to a person of a distinctly artistic and original nature. What you cannot stand is jealousy, for you have friends of both sexes and would want to keep things that way.

Venus in Pisces

The first thing people tend to notice about you is your wonderful, warm smile. Being very charitable by nature you will do anything to help others, even if you don't know them well. Much of your life may be spent sorting out situations for other people, but it is very important to feel that you are living for yourself too. In the main, you remain cheerful, and tend to be quite attractive to members of the opposite sex. Where romantic attachments are concerned, you could be drawn to people who are significantly older or younger than yourself or to someone with a unique career or point of view. It might be best for you to avoid marrying whilst you are still very young.

LIBRA:
2007 DIARY PAGES

October
2007

1 MONDAY
Moon Age Day 19   Moon Sign Gemini

You are usually very good at reaching out to others, but rarely as accomplished as proves to be the case right now. Many of your joys today come from your association with the world at large, and you can make your popularity go off the scale. There is a strong focus on individuals who come new to your life.

2 TUESDAY
Moon Age Day 20   Moon Sign Gemini

You now need to find someone with whom you can establish a more intellectual base to your thoughts and endeavours. Your own considerations and philosophical views are of supreme important but what you want the most is a good sounding board. Your attitude towards love may be slightly odd at present.

3 WEDNESDAY
Moon Age Day 21   Moon Sign Cancer

As long as you find a project that interests you, your present tenth-house Mars encourages you to stick with it. You get the most out of life at the moment by focusing your energies, and could lose out if you try to do too many different things. Try to shape up your professional life to being the way you want it.

4 THURSDAY
Moon Age Day 22   Moon Sign Cancer

Your workplace could be a breeding ground for new contacts and different interests. When you are on your own your mind runs deep and may well take you back into the distant past. There is little of any consequence there for you right now because all your potential successes lie in the present.

5 FRIDAY
Moon Age Day 23   Moon Sign Leo

Trends encourage activities at the moment that involve groups of people, and the more introspective qualities that predominated yesterday are not around now. You can afford to keep up your efforts to get a friend to try something new and if possible take them by the hand. Your consideration for others is extra noteworthy today.

6 SATURDAY
Moon Age Day 24   Moon Sign Leo

You may well have an insatiable ambition to move forward in your life generally and could be doing everything you can to enthuse others. This may be a hard job at present and there are occasions during which you will simply have to go it alone. Romance can be settled and happy for most of the weekend.

7 SUNDAY
Moon Age Day 25   Moon Sign Leo

This would be an excellent day during which to express the lighter side of your nature. You have what it takes to be both funny and appealing, so that getting others to do your bidding should be a piece of cake. If routines bore you, don't be afraid to take time out to do whatever takes your personal fancy.

8 MONDAY
Moon Age Day 26   Moon Sign Virgo

It's worth looking at your current personal circumstances as closely as you can today because there are almost certainly some slight changes to be made. You might tend to kick against doing things that are becoming slightly tedious, but if they are necessary it would be best to simply get them out of the way early in the day.

9 TUESDAY
Moon Age Day 27   Moon Sign Virgo

Whilst you have the ability to attract a significant number of admirers at the moment, it is what you feel about yourself that matters the most. You should avoid taking your need to please others too far, because in the main people like you the way you are. There is such a thing as trying too hard!

10 WEDNESDAY　　　*Moon Age Day 28*　　*Moon Sign Libra*

The Moon returns to your zodiac sign and brings with it a host of new possibilities as well as greater energy to follow your own desires. Chance your arm a little today by all means, but probably not in terms of finances. You can certainly get people to listen to your bright ideas.

11 THURSDAY　　　*Moon Age Day 0*　　*Moon Sign Libra*

Be prepared to make a positive change of some sort and to discover things about yourself that you have suspected but did not know for certain. All of that famous Air-sign energy is in place and you can use it especially well when it comes to convincing others of your skills and credentials.

12 FRIDAY　　☿　　*Moon Age Day 1*　　*Moon Sign Libra*

This is a period that could be very busy on the career front and that offers scope for you to get what you want in a material sense. You retain your enthusiasm and your sex appeal so that others could hardly fail to realise you are around. Routines are still necessary but no less tedious.

13 SATURDAY　　☿　　*Moon Age Day 2*　　*Moon Sign Scorpio*

Now you can make the most of your personal strengths. The Sun remains in your solar first house and this is definitely the time of the year during which you have chance to shine. Avoid family arguments, but put forward your point of view if you can do without upsetting anyone too much.

14 SUNDAY　　☿　　*Moon Age Day 3*　　*Moon Sign Scorpio*

Trends assist you to improve your finances around this time, and you could probably afford to treat yourself a little. You should be quite organised today, but need to be aware that there are personal matters that demand your attention. This is not a day to take on too much in a practical or a professional sense.

15 MONDAY   ☿ *Moon Age Day 4*   *Moon Sign Sagittarius*

You prove yourself to be a person who has tremendous mental gifts and can now make more headway with a particular skill than has been possible for quite some time. Energy levels remain potentially high and you needn't go short of the sort of attention that proves how much others think of you.

16 TUESDAY   ☿ *Moon Age Day 5*   *Moon Sign Sagittarius*

Your strength lies in your enthusiasm and your flair for leadership. Now you should be more than willing to embark on new enterprises and can put yourself at the head of anything you undertake. The shyer and more retiring qualities of the zodiac sign of Libra are definitely taking a holiday at this time.

17 WEDNESDAY ☿ *Moon Age Day 6*   *Moon Sign Sagittarius*

There could well be a natural nostalgia about you today and a slight reversal of some of the more positive trends that have stood around you for the last few days. Taking a break from always being at the front should offer you a chance to look carefully at life and especially at the needs of those around you.

18 THURSDAY   ☿ *Moon Age Day 7*   *Moon Sign Capricorn*

There are certain pitfalls possible today, brought about by the position of Mars in your solar tenth house. In a professional sense you still have what it takes to get ahead, but might suspect the motives of certain people and so will be more careful. It looks as though everything is in order but you are forced to wonder.

19 FRIDAY   ☿ *Moon Age Day 8*   *Moon Sign Capricorn*

The power of your personality now shines more in your social life than in any other area. Mixing with like-minded people is specifically interesting, and can benefit from stretching your intellectual capabilities to the full. Don't be afraid to attract the attention of authority figures, as their help could be valuable.

20 SATURDAY ☿ *Moon Age Day 9* *Moon Sign Aquarius*

In a career sense there is a great deal going on that you would see as being progressive, but of course this won't strike home if you don't work at the weekend. All the same you can get your head round some of the moves you will have to make to further your interests, and might be busy in other ways too.

21 SUNDAY ☿ *Moon Age Day 10* *Moon Sign Aquarius*

Trends suggest you are far more likely to play the prima donna today than at any other time this month. You have it within you to impress the right people, but could be inclined to make an opponent or two along the way. You would be wise to think before you speak, and if you are in any doubt at all, keep your counsel.

22 MONDAY ☿ *Moon Age Day 11* *Moon Sign Pisces*

Even if you plan methodically for what you want to happen, things can occur that get in the way. At work you will be able to hit targets well enough and should be in a position to make significant headway when it comes to anything new or revolutionary. What you don't have right now is a useful crystal ball!

23 TUESDAY ☿ *Moon Age Day 12* *Moon Sign Pisces*

It is time for greater financial success, but are you in the right position to make the most of the positive trends that come along? It's worth being careful about how you approach others and making certain that their interests are covered as much as your own. Your reputation is important to you, particularly at the moment.

24 WEDNESDAY ☿ *Moon Age Day 13* *Moon Sign Pisces*

Before today is out you might notice the arrival of a definite lean patch and a time during which things just don't seem to work out quite the way you would have expected. A sense of renewal is also on offer, though there may be very little you can do about this until later in the week or even at the weekend.

25 THURSDAY ☿ *Moon Age Day 14* *Moon Sign Aries*

Don't try to force issues at the moment or there's a good chance you could come unstuck. The fact is that with the lunar low about you would be much better off watching and waiting, rather than risking too much at a less than impressive period. Advice from those closest to you is there for the taking.

26 FRIDAY ☿ *Moon Age Day 15* *Moon Sign Aries*

Money matters are highlighted, but with such a negative attitude at the moment you could be less than willing to take even the simplest chance. This is no bad thing. There may be people around at the moment who definitely do not have your best interests at heart and caution is necessary, at least until tomorrow.

27 SATURDAY ☿ *Moon Age Day 16* *Moon Sign Taurus*

The general situation can now be improved. You are able to simplify your life and shouldn't be so inclined to look on the black side as you have for the last few days. Now is the time to clear away any unnecessary dead wood from your life and start thinking positively about what you can do to improve your lot generally.

28 SUNDAY ☿ *Moon Age Day 17* *Moon Sign Taurus*

In a general sense you can show yourself to be a pioneering type at the moment. Even if you don't have all the drive and enthusiasm that was the case earlier this month, you can make up for that fact with perseverance and an ability to see through potential problems. Of your startling intuition there should be no doubt.

29 MONDAY ☿ *Moon Age Day 18* *Moon Sign Gemini*

Money matters can be shaped up nicely and you might also decide to turn your attention towards matters of the heart. In any sporting activity you have what it takes to excel, not so much as a result of your physical strength but rather your skill. Attracting specific praise from others shouldn't be difficult now.

30 TUESDAY   ☿ *Moon Age Day 19   Moon Sign Gemini*

Today's trends assist you to be ambitious and capable of much self-discipline. This could be of supreme importance at work and also in terms of your social life. There are gains to be made as a result of past efforts and also thanks to the timely intervention of friends, some of whom have excellent ideas you can get them to share with you.

31 WEDNESDAY ☿   *Moon Age Day 20   Moon Sign Cancer*

There are signs that relationships change or in some cases seem to break down slightly. You might be somewhat oversensitive and do need to keep a good sense of proportion under present trends. Family members may be anxious to grab your attention, and as a result this could seem to be a very busy time.

November

2007

1 THURSDAY
☿ *Moon Age Day 21   Moon Sign Cancer*

This is an excellent period during which to remain active on the social scene. Your usual affability can be put on display and although there may be slight annoyances to be dealt with around now, in the main you can show yourself to be courteous, quick to learn and anxious to please
where possible.

2 FRIDAY
☿ *Moon Age Day 22   Moon Sign Leo*

If you have had it in mind to seek an increase in pay, you could do worse than to ask right now. The Sun has moved into your solar second house, encouraging you to deal with any outstanding debts and to get very much on the ball when it comes to your organisational skills – at home as well as at work.

3 SATURDAY
Moon Age Day 23   Moon Sign Leo

Your ability to achieve short-term goals is highlighted, as is your happy-go-lucky attitude. This would be an excellent day for setting out on a shopping spree and you may decide to do some of the inevitable Christmas shopping – only this year earlier than usual.

4 SUNDAY
Moon Age Day 24   Moon Sign Virgo

Though you are generally optimistic and filled with enthusiasm you need to assess carefully how information arriving at the moment can be put to the best use. Mercury has now entered your solar first house so communicating with those around you may be more important than any other factor.

5 MONDAY   *Moon Age Day 25   Moon Sign Virgo*

During this period you may well desire a little privacy, but this is not a situation that is likely to last very long. On the contrary, by tomorrow you should be right on the boil and so it would be sensible to get yourself ready for what lies ahead. You have what it takes to bring out the sensitive side of friends.

6 TUESDAY   *Moon Age Day 26   Moon Sign Libra*

Make the most of a day that can be especially fulfilling. Whatever you decide to do should be accomplished with little effort, and you should keep a smile on your face for most of the time. Fresh starts are indicated, and these are just as likely in your home life as they are at work.

7 WEDNESDAY   *Moon Age Day 27   Moon Sign Libra*

A high spot and a time when you can get Lady Luck to work with you. Thoughts of comfort and security are probably out of the window, particularly if you are now more than willing to take a chance and to push things further than usual. Personal attachments can be particularly rewarding, so it's worth capitalising on present trends.

8 THURSDAY   *Moon Age Day 28   Moon Sign Libra*

The lunar high continues to enhance your confidence. You have what it takes to turn an instant decision into an overnight success, and to push forward into regions of life that have been unknown to you in the past. Libra is especially creative for most of this week.

9 FRIDAY   *Moon Age Day 0   Moon Sign Scorpio*

There is still a busy feel to life, so much so that paying the attention you should to others may be quite difficult. Your strength lies in keeping as focused as possible because there are many potential distractions, one or two of which could lead you in entirely the wrong direction. Don't be frightened of your own potential success.

10 SATURDAY   *Moon Age Day 1*   *Moon Sign Scorpio*

You are so typical of your zodiac sign today, not least because you have the ability to see both sides of any situation. This is fine as far as it goes but if you want to achieve anything at the moment you will ultimately have to make a choice. Don't hesitate when decisions are necessary.

11 SUNDAY   *Moon Age Day 2*   *Moon Sign Sagittarius*

The Moon is in your solar third house, a good position when it comes to communicating your ideas to others. The slightly nostalgic phase that has been overtaking you on and off for weeks could well return now, motivating you to catapult your thoughts into the past.

12 MONDAY   *Moon Age Day 3*   *Moon Sign Sagittarius*

Financial trends assist you to ensure you are better off than you had been expecting. It could be that you have miscalculated or maybe you have simply been working that much harder of late. In terms of business this has potential to be a good time for any important decisions that have been delayed.

13 TUESDAY   *Moon Age Day 4*   *Moon Sign Sagittarius*

You cannot afford to stay at home and bury your head under a blanket, even if in some ways at least this is what you would most like to do. Don't be afraid of forcing yourself forward and making those important decisions. This week is all about committing yourself.

14 WEDNESDAY   *Moon Age Day 5*   *Moon Sign Capricorn*

Getting your own way should not be too difficult. Rather than simply settling for what seems like a compromise, why not push forward and go for gold? Routines can be a bit of a drag and there is every reason to believe you could be ringing the changes both in your working life and at home.

15 THURSDAY   *Moon Age Day 6   Moon Sign Capricorn*

The planetary emphasis is now on finance and the sense of personal security that seems to be so important to you. At the same time you are in a position to show a very original streak in your social life and might even be mixing with individuals who have not formed a part of your immediate circle before.

16 FRIDAY   *Moon Age Day 7   Moon Sign Aquarius*

You have potential to show a strongly independent streak, a fact you can put down to the position of Mars, which now occupies your solar tenth house. Now is the time to avoid putting undue strain on domestic relationships and to allow other family members to have their head. This is especially true with regard to younger people.

17 SATURDAY   *Moon Age Day 8   Moon Sign Aquarius*

Using the will-power and self-confidence at your disposal, you now have scope to take life by the scruff of the neck and to shake it into the shape you wish. This might mean having to be slightly less considerate of the needs of other people, but even Libra has to be just a little selfish once in a while.

18 SUNDAY   *Moon Age Day 9   Moon Sign Aquarius*

Trends encourage you to help others at a practical level. Little things you do for them have big consequences later on, and what you excel at the most is inspiring confidence. This is a Sunday that offers you a chance to get yourself noticed by those around you and during which you don't tend to procrastinate at all.

19 MONDAY   *Moon Age Day 10   Moon Sign Pisces*

Practical matters are well accented at the beginning of this week, and you can afford to be committed pretty much to your work. If you are engaged in full time education, now is the time you need to study harder than ever. It isn't so much what you know that counts, but rather the way you can put it across.

20 TUESDAY   *Moon Age Day 11   Moon Sign Pisces*

By tomorrow you may well be retreating into yourself more than
has been the case so far this month, but for the moment you are in
a position to be as positive and assertive as possible. If there is
something you really want, now is the time to summon up all your
cheek, to find the right person and to ask for it!

21 WEDNESDAY   *Moon Age Day 12   Moon Sign Aries*

This is a time best used as a lay-off period between more active
interludes. If you insist on knocking your head against a brick wall,
be prepared for a headache! Rather than struggling on when you
know the trends are not good, why not take some time out to look
and listen? The exercise should be well worthwhile.

22 THURSDAY   *Moon Age Day 13   Moon Sign Aries*

The continuing lunar low offers another potentially quieter day and
one during which you can continue to take stock. It might seem
that the world is not an especially friendly place, but that is only
because you are inclined to look on the black side more than usual.
Attracting concern from at least one person should be within your
power.

23 FRIDAY   *Moon Age Day 14   Moon Sign Taurus*

With Venus strong in your solar first house you can show yourself
to be charming and accessible. Anyone can talk to you about
anything now and your responses should be both considered and
positive. Contact with someone you haven't seen for a while is well
starred for today and across the weekend.

24 SATURDAY   *Moon Age Day 15   Moon Sign Taurus*

Today you have a natural instinct for analysing all situations and you
have scope to reach some quite radical conclusions as a result. Not
everyone is what they appear to be, something you might realise
now with startling clarity. Your best interests are served if you keep
your considered opinions to yourself for just a day or two longer.

25 SUNDAY   *Moon Age Day 16   Moon Sign Gemini*

This is a time during which you can afford to take moments out to broaden your social contacts. You should be popular and happy to be in just about any sort of company, just as long as it is not ignorant or vulgar. You are now at your best in any situation that motivates you to use your brain more than usual.

26 MONDAY   *Moon Age Day 17   Moon Sign Gemini*

Even if you are doing your very best to arrive at decisions that suit the greatest number of people today, you have to bear in mind that you can rarely if ever please everyone. In the main you are able to be in harmony with your surroundings, and probably won't be too anxious to upset any applecart – social or personal.

27 TUESDAY   *Moon Age Day 18   Moon Sign Cancer*

There could be increased professional responsibilities to be dealt with during this Tuesday. At the same time this could be just about the first time so far that you have turned your mind towards Christmas and what it will mean. Realising that there is still so much to do could pull you up in your tracks.

28 WEDNESDAY   *Moon Age Day 19   Moon Sign Cancer*

With your ruling planet still inhabiting the solar first house, your courtesy is highlighted, as is your candid and refreshing attitude to life. This assists you to get yourself noticed big time and to make sure that nobody will pass you over. The place to exploit these present trends is clearly at work.

29 THURSDAY   *Moon Age Day 20   Moon Sign Leo*

In many circles your present style would be considered too impulsive, though you could attract people all the same. A positive attitude on your part, coupled with a sense of necessary actions, will certainly pay dividends. Trends suggest you won't be keen to stand in any queue at the moment.

30 FRIDAY
Moon Age Day 21   Moon Sign Leo

This is an excellent time for socialising. Clubs, societies, groups and organisations of one sort or another could all grab your attention. It's worth leaving the work alone for a while today, particularly if you have been pushing yourself quite hard during November. The time is right to let your hair down!

♎ December 2007

1 SATURDAY
Moon Age Day 22   Moon Sign Virgo

A much more relaxed and pleasurable interlude now begins to unfold. You have a chance to show yourself to be extremely friendly but at the same time deep and even sensual in the right company. There is no doubt about how attractive you can make yourself to others – so much so that a little embarrassment could be the result.

2 SUNDAY
Moon Age Day 23   Moon Sign Virgo

You would be wise to avoid being too impulsive when you know that a more measured approach would please others more. You are usually good at weighing up those around you and this ability is stronger than ever now. Use it to your advantage, even if this means a little manipulation on your part.

3 MONDAY
Moon Age Day 24   Moon Sign Virgo

Stand by for a potentially quieter start to the day, though things could get busier as the afternoon wears on. There are gains to be made simply by being in the right place at the best time, and although you may not be overflowing with energy, you do know what it takes to impress someone.

4 TUESDAY
Moon Age Day 25   Moon Sign Libra

The lunar high for December gives you everything you need to get ahead in a practical sense. The only slight problem could be getting others to maintain the pace you are setting. Active and enterprising, you can afford to give yourself fully to all new projects and to show a positive response to work-related matters.

5 WEDNESDAY   *Moon Age Day 26   Moon Sign Libra*

It isn't like Libra to tempt fate, but that is exactly what you might be doing today. The signs are that you are willing to take almost any sort of chance because you know your own capabilities, and in any case the excitement of the situation is what captures your imagination. Money matters could be easier to negotiate.

6 THURSDAY   *Moon Age Day 27   Moon Sign Scorpio*

The potential for success exists in all matters to do with communication. You know what to say and have the knowing knack of getting others to do your bidding. Using a mixture of psychology and simple logic you are can even wind superiors and colleagues around your little finger.

7 FRIDAY   *Moon Age Day 28   Moon Sign Scorpio*

Even if the obligations you feel to others are slightly frustrating today, you do need to bear them in mind. They say that no man is an island, and that is particularly true in your case at the moment. If you alienate yourself from those who have it in their power to help you, the results could be tiresome.

8 SATURDAY   *Moon Age Day 29   Moon Sign Scorpio*

A slightly firmer approach to family or domestic matters can work wonders, particularly if those around you are allowing things to drift. Taking the initiative comes as second nature under present planetary trends, even if that means you rub someone else up the wrong way as a result.

9 SUNDAY   *Moon Age Day 0   Moon Sign Sagittarius*

Trends suggest a real weakness for beauty and all natural things at the moment and you may spend at least part of today staring at things open-mouthed. This is the refined side of Libra showing and is part of what makes you the sort of person you are. Don't be too quick to pass judgement about anything you can't really understand.

10 MONDAY
Moon Age Day 1   Moon Sign Sagittarius

There could well be a restlessness about you at the start of this working week and you may not take kindly to others telling you what you should be doing. You know your own routines best and will probably be anxious to follow your own ideas, especially when it comes to work.

11 TUESDAY
Moon Age Day 2   Moon Sign Capricorn

Being around your home is what appeals to you the most right now. The Moon is in your solar fourth house, helping you to achieve a better rapport with loved ones. This could be the time to put right something that has been going wrong recently and to achieve a greater understanding generally.

12 WEDNESDAY
Moon Age Day 3   Moon Sign Capricorn

You could now have a chance to discover some news that is significant and even heart-warming. There is a practical element to everything you do but it is quite feasible to mix business with pleasure. Romance is well starred for the evening, and social trends are gradually looking better.

13 THURSDAY
Moon Age Day 4   Moon Sign Capricorn

You have what it takes to be the personality of the moment, and to show a positive face to life, especially in a social sense. Maybe you already have your Christmas head on and are quite anxious to get arrangements of the festive period well in hand. That's fine, though you would be wise to avoid getting tied down with unnecessary details.

14 FRIDAY
Moon Age Day 5   Moon Sign Aquarius

You can use your natural generosity to attract a good deal of attention, though you need to keep your eye on expenditure. It's all very well splashing money about but you are going to need quite a lot before this month is out. Make sure the assistance you give is in kind, not in cash.

15 SATURDAY   *Moon Age Day 6   Moon Sign Aquarius*

Communication and curiosity strike home in equal quantities. If you want to know what makes the world tick, be prepared to look into every nook and cranny in your search for answers. New hobbies or pastimes could well be grabbing your attention, and you can afford to show your creative side at every opportunity.

16 SUNDAY   *Moon Age Day 7   Moon Sign Pisces*

Trends emphasise duty on this Sunday. It could be that family members are relying on you heavily and you won't want to let them down. You can best avoid rows by explaining yourself fully, and you shouldn't be afraid to allow younger family members to have more responsibility regarding their own lives.

17 MONDAY   *Moon Age Day 8   Moon Sign Pisces*

Money could be slightly easier to come by now, though it may disappear as quickly as it appears. There's a danger that you are a little too lavish for your own good and you do need to stay focused. It may be that Christmas seems like a bottomless pit into which cash is being thrown, but it doesn't have to be that way.

18 TUESDAY   *Moon Age Day 9   Moon Sign Aries*

As the lunar low arrives, you would be wise to guard against negative thinking. It would be a mistake to let any vital information pass you by, so it is important to keep looking and listening. If someone is in a very good position to offer you invaluable assistance, it isn't much use if you fail to notice the fact.

19 WEDNESDAY   *Moon Age Day 10   Moon Sign Aries*

You might decide it is now time to let go of the traces for a few hours and to allow others to do the driving. The lunar low is inclined to make you feel less positive and could also sap your strength significantly. It isn't that anything specific is likely to go wrong, merely that it's difficult for you to be quite as positive as you have been of late.

20 THURSDAY   *Moon Age Day 11   Moon Sign Taurus*

Persuasive and communicative, you must still guard against negative thinking, but you do have a greater set of incentives and should find it child's play to get others to follow your lead. As the day goes on you have a chance to discover more and more that pleases you and to make yourself attractive to those around you.

21 FRIDAY   *Moon Age Day 12   Moon Sign Taurus*

This would be a great time to work on those relationships that are most important to you. Understanding people's motivations shouldn't be difficult, and you have what it takes to see clear to the heart of any matter. This is Libra at its best and there isn't any doubt about your desire to do what you think is right when it matters the most.

22 SATURDAY   *Moon Age Day 13   Moon Sign Gemini*

Make the most of a financial boost that is going to help you follow your own plans once the New Year gets underway. At the moment this might represent little more than a promise, but it proves to be good news all the same. What it means beyond anything else is that those in positions of authority have confidence in you.

23 SUNDAY   *Moon Age Day 14   Moon Sign Gemini*

You may not want to venture too far today, and with Christmas only a couple of days away it is likely that you will find a great deal to do around home. If you have to sally forth, maybe to get those last presents, make sure you are in the company of people you love to have around you.

24 MONDAY   *Moon Age Day 15   Moon Sign Cancer*

You have scope to get things working out reasonably well for you, particularly if you are working on Christmas Eve. Getting things to slot into place should be easy enough and you can afford to show a great deal of respect for those with whom you work. A frenetic and none too comfortable atmosphere at home is indicated.

25 TUESDAY   *Moon Age Day 16   Moon Sign Cancer*

Christmas Day is very much influenced by little Mercury, which is now in your solar fourth house. This suggests that most of the really important communicating that is going on will be with people you care for greatly. Speaking words of love to your partner ought not to be a problem under present influences.

26 WEDNESDAY   *Moon Age Day 17   Moon Sign Leo*

You have a good knack for dealing with different sorts of people today and show great adaptability. There is a slight restlessness around you and that means you might be happier to be on the move, rather than sitting in a chair and toasting your toes in front of the fire. Even party games could bore you now!

27 THURSDAY   *Moon Age Day 18   Moon Sign Leo*

Emotional ties prove to be very powerful and this is a time when personal attachments mean the most. You still have what it takes to be active and enterprising, so could well be looking for excitement. However, today works best if you share adventures with your partner or else family members you look upon with great affection.

28 FRIDAY   *Moon Age Day 19   Moon Sign Leo*

The focus is on tying up loose ends today and getting yourself ready for the end of the year bash. Resolutions could well come into your mind but you need to keep these as realistic as proves to be possible. Don't be too keen to alter anything today but rather keep your planning head on.

29 SATURDAY   *Moon Age Day 20   Moon Sign Virgo*

Despite looking and feeling good, Libra could nevertheless be somewhat quieter today. This is because the Moon has entered your solar twelfth house. Rather than dwelling on situations you can't alter, your best option is to give your mind to matters that are within your power to influence. New activities have much to offer later in the day.

30 SUNDAY
Moon Age Day 21   Moon Sign Virgo

There is likely to be much happening within your life at the moment that encourages you to put a smile on your face. This is especially true as far as personal attachments are concerned. You can show yourself to be impressive and sexy, so much so that you could be attracting some attention you don't really want.

31 MONDAY
Moon Age Day 22   Moon Sign Libra

There is inspirational news on offer for the last day of the year. In addition you should have great energy at your disposal and a determination to have a good time. The fact is that the lunar high motivates you to give everything you can to life, and you could hardly be in a better state of mind to face the inevitable New Year party.

LIBRA:
2008 DIARY PAGES

LIBRA:
2008 IN BRIEF

Right from the very start of this year you will be keen to do more to lift yourself higher and further than you have managed before. You should be breaking down barriers, establishing new relationships and working hard towards preferred objectives. January and February should be both interesting and inspiring, even if you have to cope with people who are not always quite as helpful as you might wish.

As March arrives you may be running out of steam slightly and you will need the support that comes from colleagues and friends. There won't be any real problem, just a slight lack of energy and less confidence in your own abilities. The balance will soon be redressed, especially by personal attachments, which look both secure and exciting throughout the spring. April may see you prospering as a result of both limited speculation and new responsibilities.

Despite the fact that you are from an autumn-born zodiac sign, Libra loves the early summer, which is one reason why you will welcome the month of May with open arms. It is likely to be a month of fresh starts for you and a time during which you are doing your spring-cleaning, both at home and inside your head. June sees you keen to get ahead, and your nature becomes slightly prickly if you think anyone is trying to hold you back. It is July and August that are likely to see you at your most active. Not only is this likely to be a time of travel, but you may also be thinking about a change of job, alterations at home and forming new friendships. Only your love life seems to be fairly settled during this period, and even here young-at-heart Librans may well be forming a new attachment that looks significant.

If there is one part of the year during which you need to make sure you don't lose touch with reality it is during September and October. There are gains to be made, particularly in October, but both months will see you somewhat confused on occasion and less inclined to make quick decisions. This is not the best time for speculation but ought to be excellent for all home-based ventures. Most Librans also show a more competitive and sporting attitude in October.

November and December should be settled, happy and in the main successful. You end the year with surplus energy and with new incentives surrounding you. You will need to watch what you are spending during December but personal gains compensate for any financial shortfall. Christmas should be particularly memorable and there will be no doubting your popularity. Your sense of fun will be limitless as the year ends.

January 2008

1 TUESDAY
Moon Age Day 23 Moon Sign Libra

What a way to start a New Year. The Moon remains in your own zodiac sign of Libra, offering boundless energy and a burning desire to begin the year as you mean to go on. You can make sure there is fun and frivolity all round – that is if you can get anyone out of bed after last night's parties!

2 WEDNESDAY
Moon Age Day 24 Moon Sign Libra

If you are still firing on all cylinders, you should be able to find ways to get ahead of the crowd. Most important of all is your naturally cheerful attitude to life – amplified by the position of the Moon. At work you can afford to try out new ideas and to enlist the support of colleagues who could be useful to your plans.

3 THURSDAY
Moon Age Day 25 Moon Sign Scorpio

A more dynamic and self-assured Libran can now address the needs of a brand new period. There are times when you can be hesitant and you are well known for jumping around from foot to foot regarding decisions, but this shouldn't be the case at all right now. Your ability to make up your mind instantly could surprise others and astonish you.

4 FRIDAY
Moon Age Day 26 Moon Sign Scorpio

Try to get as much variety as possible into your life today and end the first working week of the year on a high if you can. Social matters are well accented, and you can use this period to address new incentives and activities both now and across the upcoming weekend.

5 SATURDAY   *Moon Age Day 27 Moon Sign Sagittarius*

What you can use to set yourself apart at the moment is your deep and sincere compassion for others. This is always present but is especially well marked under present planetary trends. Not only could you be doing all you can for family members and friends, but you can extend your naturally kind nature to just about anyone you meet today.

6 SUNDAY   *Moon Age Day 28 Moon Sign Sagittarius*

There might be the odd drawback today, possibly brought about by the slightly negative attitude of family members or your partner. You will have to find ways in which to accommodate the fact and that could put some pressure on you. However, in the main you can take life in your stride and remain as cheerful as usual.

7 MONDAY   *Moon Age Day 29 Moon Sign Sagittarius*

Love life and social issues are generally well highlighted for the moment, and with some strong incentives coming in from outside you should also be looking favourably upon new work plans and responsibilities. Even if almost everyone you know seems equally helpful today, in reality it is your own attitude that makes things swing.

8 TUESDAY   *Moon Age Day 0 Moon Sign Capricorn*

Trends still support your light-hearted frame of mind in which you don't make heavy weather of the odd difficulty that life seems to throw in your path. On the contrary, you now have what it takes to turn a difficulty into a real advantage – and all because of your extraordinary ability to look at all situations from an alternative angle.

9 WEDNESDAY   *Moon Age Day 1 Moon Sign Capricorn*

Family matters should be especially well accented now, encouraging you to spend less time attending to things outside your home and more on those you love. You might decide to do something particularly special and important for a younger family member, but such is your giving nature that this should be no trouble to you.

10 THURSDAY
Moon Age Day 2 Moon Sign Aquarius

Today the main focus is on the practical world, particularly if there are demands coming in from a number of different directions. Life remains interesting but there could be a few frustrations around. Your strength lies in being able to deal with these at present.

11 FRIDAY
Moon Age Day 3 Moon Sign Aquarius

Inspiring others shouldn't be hard for you right now, though you may not always have quite the level of confidence that appears to be the case. Never mind, what really matters is that you can convince the world at large that you know what you are doing. That's all it really takes, because when you need assistance you can certainly attract it.

12 SATURDAY
Moon Age Day 4 Moon Sign Pisces

Be prepared to show the world what you are made of this weekend, but be prepared to turn away from everyday responsibilities and towards your social life, which is now strongly emphasised. Find new ways to have fun and make sure that you include as many people as possible in your plans. Communication is the key.

13 SUNDAY
Moon Age Day 5 Moon Sign Pisces

Now is the time to approach any problems from a very different point of perspective than the one you have been adopting recently. Even if not everyone seems to be equally helpful today, it's worth asking a very special friend for support. Keep up the pressure to enhance your social and family life today.

14 MONDAY
Moon Age Day 6 Moon Sign Pisces

It would be sensible today to get as many outstanding jobs done as you can. The reason for this is the two-day period that stands ahead of you during which it might be much harder to get anything done in a concrete sense. By all means clear the decks for action but don't expect a great deal until rather later in the week.

15 TUESDAY
Moon Age Day 7   Moon Sign Aries

There are a few setbacks possible for today and tomorrow. This is because the Moon has now entered Aries, which is your opposite zodiac sign. Known as the lunar low, this period comes once each month and is the time during which you would be wise to recharge your batteries rather than to push forward with new incentives.

16 WEDNESDAY
Moon Age Day 8   Moon Sign Aries

You may decide there isn't much point in starting anything new for the moment. On the contrary, it's worth consolidating your present position and doing only those things that make your life more comfortable and secure. However, this doesn't prevent you from planning ahead, and if you have time on your hands that would be an ideal option.

17 THURSDAY
Moon Age Day 9   Moon Sign Taurus

Back to normal you can be happily on the go today and can get your head around thoughts of movement and travel. Whether you will actually be taking a trip right now is debatable, but since you will want to get all details sorted out first, you can at least deal with the practicalities of a future journey. It's worth asking friends for support.

18 FRIDAY
Moon Age Day 10   Moon Sign Taurus

There is now a strong emphasis on pleasure, assisting you to find new ways in which to feel more comfortable and secure. Part of this is down to relationships and you can be sure that this would be an ideal time to bury the hatchet over some issue that has already been going on far too long. Why not take the initiative and put things right?

19 SATURDAY
Moon Age Day 11   Moon Sign Gemini

Make the most of progressive trends at the moment by following up on all possibilities. This is not a good period for leaving things to chance or for relying on the good offices of others, no matter how well intentioned they may be. The only person you can absolutely rely on for today is you.

20 SUNDAY   *Moon Age Day 12 Moon Sign Gemini*

You can make use of great enthusiasm and enterprise at present, and have what it takes to show people a good time. Romance is especially well highlighted under today's planetary trends, making this the sort of Sunday during which you can sweep someone off their feet. This applies even if you have known the person for years.

21 MONDAY   *Moon Age Day 13 Moon Sign Cancer*

The focus is on working in large groups, and you will be at your best when it is possible to co-operate with as many individuals as possible. Even if something that seemed to be nearing completion now gets much more complicated, you needn't let this faze you at a time when you are so energetic.

22 TUESDAY   *Moon Age Day 14 Moon Sign Cancer*

All practical matters fall under your personal spotlight today and you have the precision to get things right, even jobs that have been particularly tiresome or difficult in the past. You have scope to attract accolades from more than one direction, and to make yourself the flavour of the month with many.

23 WEDNESDAY   *Moon Age Day 15 Moon Sign Leo*

Don't give in right now, even if the odds seem to be stacked against you. If you persevere there is no end to the successes you can enjoy, and what is more you can get nearly all the support you need. 'Nearly' is the operative word because one or two people could be somewhat difficult to predict around this time.

24 THURSDAY   *Moon Age Day 16 Moon Sign Leo*

Such is your intuition that you are likely to know instinctively who you can trust to get it right first time – or indeed any time. If some individuals seem determined to be difficult, your best response is to leave them to their own devices, whilst you get on and move towards some important milestones.

25 FRIDAY
Moon Age Day 17 Moon Sign Virgo

The Moon is now in your solar twelfth house, encouraging a slightly quieter interlude than has been the case recently. There is time to think and to plan, as well as plenty of moments to spend with your partner or family members. The time is right to let everyone know how much you care about them and to be especially kind to friends.

26 SATURDAY
Moon Age Day 18 Moon Sign Virgo

With the arrival of the weekend you have what it takes to get things moving the way you would wish. Take care though because you may not be at your most dynamic for today, and even if there is something inside you that yearns for activity and excitement, it is likely to be tomorrow before your body catches up with your brain.

27 SUNDAY
Moon Age Day 19 Moon Sign Libra

Swift progress can now become a reality and the lunar high offers any number of new incentives, plus the energy you need to follow things through. The lunar high will still be around as you embark on a new working week and it is very important to get things straight in your mind in order to use its power to the full tomorrow.

28 MONDAY
Moon Age Day 20 Moon Sign Libra

You now have potential to achieve both personal and professional aims and should not be held back just because others think the time is right to slow things down. On the contrary, if people don't want to keep up – or cannot do so – you can plough your own furrow and leave them to their own devices for now.

29 TUESDAY ☿
Moon Age Day 21 Moon Sign Libra

You continue to be able to show your most dynamic and potentially successful face to the world at large, and what really shines out at the moment is your increasing popularity. This allows you to develop a greater degree of confidence. Creative potential is very good now.

30 WEDNESDAY ☿   *Moon Age Day 22   Moon Sign Scorpio*

There is a definite restless side to your nature under present planetary trends, and a slight irritability if others don't have the same ideas that are occurring to you. For once Libra wants to do everything its own way, which may well be a cause of some surprise to those who know you are generally compliant.

31 THURSDAY ☿   *Moon Age Day 23   Moon Sign Scorpio*

Be prepared to welcome new personalities into your life around now, and to get the best out of what they can offer you. At the same time your own ingenuity is highlighted, and you can get colleagues especially to follow paths that you indicate. Share the load today and don't overwork.

February
2008

1 FRIDAY
☿ *Moon Age Day 24 Moon Sign Sagittarius*

You can start the new month in a very energetic frame of mind, but it is possible that the demands life makes of you could be rather too severe. For this reason it would be sensible to pace yourself and to avoid getting bogged down with too many details. An across-the-board approach to life now works better than too much concentration.

2 SATURDAY
☿ *Moon Age Day 25 Moon Sign Sagittarius*

From a social point of view you can afford to be in a very positive frame of mind and to fall in line with just about anything that your partner or friends wishes to do. This is Libra at its most compliant, and you may decide to shelve your own plans in order to accommodate something new and original.

3 SUNDAY
☿ *Moon Age Day 26 Moon Sign Sagittarius*

Your ability to impress people is very noticeable today and you can put yourself in exactly the right position to draw the most from life in almost every way. Some of your personal ambitions might be rather grandiose, but with a little time and thought you can sculpt these into more modest and therefore achievable objectives.

4 MONDAY
☿ *Moon Age Day 27 Moon Sign Capricorn*

The focus is on your personal ambitions at the moment, and you may be working as fast as you can today in order to get everything done. Actually there might not be quite the panic you think, and you might achieve more if you slow down somewhat – but tell that to a Libran who is on the move!

5 TUESDAY ☿ *Moon Age Day 28 Moon Sign Capricorn*

You still have scope to get a great deal done, and may not have too much patience with anyone who is unwilling to keep up your pace. Once the work is out of the way you can drop back to being your usual, easy-going self, and increase your popularity with others by being willing to listen to what they are really saying.

6 WEDNESDAY ☿ *Moon Age Day 0 Moon Sign Aquarius*

Trends suggest that your spirits are raised and you shouldn't have any difficulty at all getting your partner or other family members into the same sort of mood that presently surrounds you. Don't be too quick to criticise a colleague today. Instead, why not look ahead and make sure your own progress will be smooth?

7 THURSDAY ☿ *Moon Age Day 1 Moon Sign Aquarius*

You certainly needn't shrink into the background at present, and have what it takes to stand out there alone in the spotlight. This is fine just as long as there are not too many decisions to be made, because it is at this point that Libra sometimes experiences a degree of difficulty. Still, you can at least look super-confident.

8 FRIDAY ☿ *Moon Age Day 2 Moon Sign Aquarius*

Now is the best time to assess what is really going on in your life and to make a few alterations if you think they are necessary. It might be prudent to dump something now, before it turns out to be a real handicap to you. Being born of an Air sign like Libra, you don't care for carrying too much baggage in any case.

9 SATURDAY ☿ *Moon Age Day 3 Moon Sign Pisces*

Dealing with authority figures could take up at least a part of your Saturday, particularly if you don't get all the answers you would wish. You might have to be somewhat more dominant than usual, and even if you don't want to cause a scene – which you hate – you do have the right to a fair crack of the whip.

10 SUNDAY ☿ *Moon Age Day 4 Moon Sign Pisces*

A day to keep plugging away and if possible get a few necessary tasks out of the way because there are somewhat quieter times ahead. For the moment you remain energetic, filled with optimism and more than able to make a good impression when it counts. Look out for unusual reactions from others.

11 MONDAY ☿ *Moon Age Day 5 Moon Sign Aries*

The Moon returns to your opposite zodiac sign of Aries, bringing the lunar low for February. This has potential to be a much quieter interlude, though it can be one you can relish rather than hate. Everyone needs a few moments now and again during which they can collect themselves and think. Libra is no exception.

12 TUESDAY ☿ *Moon Age Day 6 Moon Sign Aries*

Trends herald another run-of-the-mill sort of day when there may not be too much excitement about. Avoid taking chances at the moment, especially with money. Your best approach is to keep all your dealings transparent and honest. Colleagues could prove difficult to deal with but part of the problem may be coming from you.

13 WEDNESDAY ☿ *Moon Age Day 7 Moon Sign Taurus*

A work issue could need some urgent attention, so be prepared to get back on form and looking at things with a greater sense of both urgency and optimism. Some timely actions early in the day might save you a good deal of time and trouble later, and there is certainly truth for you now in the adage 'strike whilst the iron is hot'.

14 THURSDAY ☿ *Moon Age Day 8 Moon Sign Taurus*

Along comes a very noticeable phase during which your powers of attraction are heightened considerably. At work you could discover that you are almost psychic in your ability to read situations quickly and accurately, and your powers of discrimination have rarely been better than they appear to be right now.

15 FRIDAY ☿ *Moon Age Day 9 Moon Sign Gemini*

It's time to project yourself, and the chance to do so is probably more accented in the professional arena than in any other sphere of your life. All the same you can be very sociably inclined and today offers the chance to mix business with pleasure. Be careful you don't inadvertently upset your partner or an older relative.

16 SATURDAY ☿ *Moon Age Day 10 Moon Sign Gemini*

Once more you can get yourself in the best possible position to further your own cause and to feed one or two of your long-term desires. In matters of love Libra can be red hot at present, and your simmering passions shouldn't be lost on the right people. This could be a weekend to remember for those of you who are looking for a new love.

17 SUNDAY ☿ *Moon Age Day 11 Moon Sign Cancer*

A day to take advantage of friendly and well-intentioned assistance, even if you are rather suspicious in some cases. When you are not busy with everyday chores at present you can find fascinating ways in which to entertain yourself and have the means to bring joy to others too.

18 MONDAY ☿ *Moon Age Day 12 Moon Sign Cancer*

Trends suggest there might be problems emerging when it comes to getting on with other people. Even if your associates are acting in ways that surprise and sometimes upset you, too great a reaction is not to be recommended. It's shock value that people are looking for, so why not defuse the situation by staying cool?

19 TUESDAY ☿ *Moon Age Day 13 Moon Sign Leo*

You are clearly more susceptible to outside influence right now, so beware of taking too much advice from friends. In the end you would be much better off finding a quiet corner where you can think things through and come to your own conclusions. Although the answers you come to may be radical, they are at least yours.

20 WEDNESDAY   *Moon Age Day 14 Moon Sign Leo*

The focus is now on your response to people in positions of
authority, particularly if they are lording it over everyone today. It
would be sensible to avoid too much reaction and to simply watch
and wait. Your time will come and when it does you need to act
rationally and coolly.

21 THURSDAY   *Moon Age Day 15 Moon Sign Leo*

Though you thrive on life and love to keep up a fairly hectic pace,
you could find that you will get on much better today if you actively
slow things down. This shouldn't be a problem at all on Friday and
Saturday, but for the moment there are many pressures urging you
on and turning down any opportunity may not be at all easy.

22 FRIDAY   *Moon Age Day 16 Moon Sign Virgo*

The Moon is now in your solar twelfth house, offering the chance
of a quieter interlude than has been the case for the last few days.
Instead of constantly pushing forward, it's worth slowing down the
pace of life considerably. Take a walk today, or maybe make a trip to
a place that is very special to you.

23 SATURDAY   *Moon Age Day 17 Moon Sign Virgo*

It is the things that others are saying and doing that can have the
most profound part to play in your thinking during the first part of
this weekend. If you are quieter you are also more inclined to listen,
and this offers you scope to gather new information. People really
like you at present and should say so.

24 SUNDAY   *Moon Age Day 18 Moon Sign Libra*

It's time to get busy with major initiatives, though with the first day
of the lunar high falling on a Sunday, you might find it hard to move
forward in a professional sense. When it comes to excitement,
diversity and a desire to travel you can now be the number one. Such
is your magnetism that you can persuade others to follow your lead.

84

25 MONDAY
Moon Age Day 19 Moon Sign Libra

New ideas in the business arena count for a great deal at the moment, and you also have what it takes to turn your attention in the direction of your home. The time is right to make quite significant changes, and you needn't let anything prevent you from doing so around now.

26 TUESDAY
Moon Age Day 20 Moon Sign Scorpio

Don't let good ideas fall by the wayside just because you are too busy to deal with them right now. If necessary you need to get a pad and pen so that you can write down what you are thinking. That way you can come back to these plans at a later date and will end up being extremely happy that you made a note of them.

27 WEDNESDAY
Moon Age Day 21 Moon Sign Scorpio

It's worth looking to friends and trusted relatives for advice – that is if you feel the need of any. Actually you may not be half so confident in your own abilities at the moment as would often be the case, so a little timely reassurance would work wonders. Libra often jumps about from foot to foot, but that's something you should avoid today.

28 THURSDAY
Moon Age Day 22 Moon Sign Scorpio

This may be a time of new and unexpected domestic obligations, some of which could bore the pants off you. Maybe you should find ways to get others involved, so that you are not working on your own. Doing this allows you to change the whole complexion of the situation and make a boring chore into a fascinating social adventure.

29 FRIDAY
Moon Age Day 23 Moon Sign Sagittarius

There are times to speak your mind and other periods when it would be much more sensible to wait and see. Today is such a period, and present planetary trends say 'watch and wait'. Don't be too surprised if some sort of celebrity pays a visit to your life around now, and a little fame of your own may be just a telephone call away.

March

2008

1 SATURDAY
Moon Age Day 24 Moon Sign Sagittarius

Getting ahead now is just a matter of adopting the right point of view, and also a case of showing that even compliant Libra can be stubborn when it matters. If you let people take you for granted, perhaps you should not be too surprised when that is exactly what they do. Stand up for yourself today – but with a good sense of humour too.

2 SUNDAY
Moon Age Day 25 Moon Sign Capricorn

You may feel the need to be freed from all restrictions at the start of this week and won't take too kindly to anyone who appears to be taking your freedom and independence away. In reality certain individuals really are trying to help you, but it may be difficult to appreciate the fact from your present point of perspective.

3 MONDAY
Moon Age Day 26 Moon Sign Capricorn

There isn't much wrong with your cognitive powers at present, and working out how to get on well should be quite easy. It is only when it comes to personal attachments that you might be somewhat blind to situations. Confidence to do the right thing is present, but you might have to search inside yourself if you want to find it.

4 TUESDAY
Moon Age Day 27 Moon Sign Capricorn

If life seems to be testing you today, you can at least be sure that you have what it takes to pass the examination. Superiors especially might be keeping an eye on you, but this is very unlikely to be because they are dissatisfied with your performance. On the contrary, you have potential to attract the most positive sort of attention right now.

5 WEDNESDAY   *Moon Age Day 28 Moon Sign Aquarius*

Opportunities for progress lie around every corner, even if it might seem as though you need a periscope to see them. Fortunately you have great insight into the behaviour of others and a good deal of intuition at the moment. Take these, add a little common sense, and it seems as though you have the best recipe for success.

6 THURSDAY   *Moon Age Day 29 Moon Sign Aquarius*

Life shakes things up a little, sometimes without any input at all from you. Take things in your stride and don't be upset if you are put on the spot. If ever there was a person who can rise to the task it is you, and what is more you have what it takes to fulfil all expectations of you whilst wearing a cheery smile on your face.

7 FRIDAY   *Moon Age Day 0 Moon Sign Pisces*

Even if you want to be at the forefront of things from a social perspective, there may be jobs that need to be done first. This can turn out to be rather frustrating, particularly if you jog along from one rather tedious task to another. Nevertheless if you persevere you should find part of the day that you can truly call your own.

8 SATURDAY   *Moon Age Day 1 Moon Sign Pisces*

There are signs that not all of the responses you get today are going to be equally warm or welcome. For this reason you would be wise to stick to those individuals who quite clearly think you are flavour of the month. Getting involved in arguments with the other sort of people is simply a waste of time today.

9 SUNDAY   *Moon Age Day 2 Moon Sign Aries*

The time is right to slow things down a little now, and with the Moon back in Aries you need to be rather circumspect about what you take on today. Spring is on the way and the weather should be improving just a little. Why not get out of doors and enjoy the lengthening days? On the way you could well meet the odd entertaining individual.

10 MONDAY   *Moon Age Day 3 Moon Sign Aries*

Putting yourself at the forefront of things in a social sense shouldn't be too difficult at present, though there could be a slower than average pace professionally. The lunar low discourages you from making some of the connections that will be possible in a day or two and may also convince you to compromise more.

11 TUESDAY   *Moon Age Day 4 Moon Sign Taurus*

This is a time for togetherness in at least one sense. The focus is now on home and family, and you may be quite happy to spend some time doing domestic things, rather than trying to push ahead all the time in the outside world. An ideal time to make contact with someone you don't see very often.

12 WEDNESDAY   *Moon Age Day 5 Moon Sign Taurus*

Your sensitivity to others is much enhanced under present planetary trends, and if you did something slightly wrong in a relationship sense at the weekend you can put it right today. Rather than getting tied down with details at work why not take an overview of as many situations as you can? This works best for Libra at present.

13 THURSDAY   *Moon Age Day 6 Moon Sign Gemini*

If there is something you really want to get done, do it today! Your organisational skills are favoured, and you should recognise instinctively when it is the best time to act. There may be moments right now when some of the details of life pass you by, but it is possible for you to find useful short cuts to your objectives.

14 FRIDAY   *Moon Age Day 7 Moon Sign Gemini*

It may seem as though others are lacking some of the sensitivity that you are taking as second nature within yourself at present, but you can't expect everyone to be alike. If the attitude of anyone bothers you, it's worth leaving them alone for a while and concentrating on individuals who do inspire you and with whom you can establish a rapport.

15 SATURDAY
Moon Age Day 8 Moon Sign Cancer

You have scope to get partnerships working out well for you now, and this could be particularly true in the case of business associations. Although the weekend might not be the best time for making professional decisions, the trends are so good that you might make an exception. Meanwhile family members may well amuse you.

16 SUNDAY
Moon Age Day 9 Moon Sign Cancer

There is no doubt about your ability to be in the right place to lend a helping hand at present, but there's nothing especially unusual about that for Libra. What might be different is the way you choose to offer assistance right now. You may well decide to do so from a distance and in a way that prevents others from realising what you are up to.

17 MONDAY
Moon Age Day 10 Moon Sign Cancer

You could do a lot worse today than getting together with someone you love in congenial surroundings and enjoying yourself whilst others are toiling away. If this isn't possible all through today, you might have to make do with the evening instead. Some fresh air would work wonders today, even if it's only for a few minutes.

18 TUESDAY
Moon Age Day 11 Moon Sign Leo

Libra should be on a roll at present, helping you to find the answer to all sorts of little problems almost instinctively. There is little doubt about your popularity and you will recognise only too well when someone is giving you the come-on. Whether you take any notice or not, these situations can boost your ego.

19 WEDNESDAY·
Moon Age Day 12 Moon Sign Leo

The things that others do on your behalf help you to feel rather special at the moment, and this can be a fairly smooth-running and enjoyable period for nearly all Libran subjects. If there are any difficulties at present these are likely to come from the direction of your family and are as a result of your tendency to worry too much.

20 THURSDAY   *Moon Age Day 13 Moon Sign Virgo*

Trends suggest you won't be lacking in social graces today and can be more than trusted to put on a good show when it matters the most. Almost anyone you meet at the moment can prove to be of use to you in one way or another, and you have what it takes to persuade them that you are exclusively helping them along.

21 FRIDAY   *Moon Age Day 14 Moon Sign Virgo*

Even if things are slightly quieter whilst the Moon passes through your solar twelfth house, you do have what it takes to make a good impression on colleagues or superiors at work. The time is right to work steadily towards your objectives without making a fuss or being too brash. It's your professionalism that really gets you noticed now.

22 SATURDAY   *Moon Age Day 15 Moon Sign Libra*

The Moon returns to Libra and brings with it one of the most reactive and potentially exciting periods during March. Now is the time to push on with your objectives, and Libra certainly shouldn't be taking no for an answer today. By all means give yourself a pat on the back for a particular success, but don't wait around to gloat. There's more to do.

23 SUNDAY   *Moon Age Day 16 Moon Sign Libra*

You shouldn't be lacking in optimism when it matters the most, and can show just about everyone today just how organised and successful you can be. Some of your efforts are made now for periods well into the future, but you can gain a great deal of personal satisfaction from most areas of your life.

24 MONDAY   *Moon Age Day 17 Moon Sign Libra*

What a way to begin a new working week!?If you are still on a roll, you might push yourself forward much more than might normally be the case. You can use this to attract deference from others and to get them to follow your lead in most circumstances. You can afford to take time out later in the day to help a friend.

25 TUESDAY *Moon Age Day 18 Moon Sign Scorpio*

Make good use of your very astute mind today and learn that not everything comes to you as a result of effort but sometimes thanks to pure good luck. If you fail to realise this fact something of potentially great importance could pass you by, and that would be a great pity. Don't get involved in family rows, but as usual sort them out.

26 WEDNESDAY *Moon Age Day 19 Moon Sign Scorpio*

News that comes to you via colleagues or friends could be of great importance so it is really sensible to keep your ears open today. In the main you shouldn't miss a trick, and show yourself to be alert and very reactive. You may also be just a little touchy on occasions, and should be willing to count to ten before losing your temper.

27 THURSDAY *Moon Age Day 20 Moon Sign Sagittarius*

It's possible that not everything goes strictly the way you would wish. That needn't matter at all if you keep an open mind and show yourself able to ride with the ups and downs as if you were on a roller coaster. If people you love are depending on you, be prepared to think rather carefully before offering them some timely advice.

28 FRIDAY *Moon Age Day 21 Moon Sign Sagittarius*

This potentially fulfilling period in relationships comes about mostly as a result of the position of Venus in your solar chart. You are somewhat realistic in your approach to love, but still have what it takes to sweep someone off their feet. This evening is almost certainly the right time to make overtures to a new love.

29 SATURDAY *Moon Age Day 22 Moon Sign Sagittarius*

Make the most of a very harmonious period in personal matters and also recognise just how much a new friendship is adding to your life. New personalities are on the horizon all the time and they bring with them different ways of looking at existing situations. This is a day during which you can afford to spend time on yourself.

30 SUNDAY   *Moon Age Day 23   Moon Sign Capricorn*

Libra can be very romantically inclined at the moment and the fact shows itself in a number of different ways. Your naturally warm nature should be appreciated by everyone, and you have scope to show just how zany and excitable Libra can be. There are moments right now when you could get away with saying almost anything!

31 MONDAY   *Moon Age Day 24   Moon Sign Capricorn*

For Libra it is so often the case that love makes the world go round, and current trends support this. You can be warm, sincere, open and funny, which just about sums up the best traits of your zodiac sign. However, there is also a significant depth to your thinking at present which can gain you recognition and respect from others.

April
2008

1 TUESDAY
Moon Age Day 25 Moon Sign Aquarius

There is plenty of concentration available to you today, and if there is one particular job that has been demanding your attention for some time now, today is right for getting it sorted altogether. Libra can also be very intuitive under present planetary trends, and you can be sure that your feelings regarding someone else are quite accurate.

2 WEDNESDAY
Moon Age Day 26 Moon Sign Aquarius

Don't let things get tense today and especially not within your family. If there are some touchy people about, you will have to deal with them whether you like it or not. The attitude of colleagues can be puzzling, but it's worth considering that they may be jealous of you in ways you could hardly comprehend.

3 THURSDAY
Moon Age Day 27 Moon Sign Pisces

Confidence remains in place, even when you are dealing with situations you don't entirely understand. You give your best at work but will be really in your element once responsibilities are out of the way and you can enjoy yourself in congenial company. With the spring now in full flow, you need plenty of fresh air.

4 FRIDAY
Moon Age Day 28 Moon Sign Pisces

Once again you have a chance to demonstrate just how understanding and kind Libra can be. Even when someone has given you a hard time in the past you should be quite willing to forgive and forget. This is a very fortunate attitude because burying the hatchet now can prove to be of tremendous use to you in the days and weeks to come.

93

5 SATURDAY
Moon Age Day 29 Moon Sign Pisces

There can be a few obstacles about today, possibly from some fairly surprising directions. The Moon is moving on towards Aries and so by the end of today you might be feeling a little pressured and less motivated than was the case only yesterday. New incentives may be hard to find between now and Tuesday.

6 SUNDAY
Moon Age Day 0 Moon Sign Aries

It could seem as though your plans are blocked in all directions and you will need to think very carefully before acting today. The lunar low does nothing to promote the fire and vivacity that you would really need in order to make significant progress, and you could feel as though you are also failing to show your usual common sense.

7 MONDAY
Moon Age Day 1 Moon Sign Aries

As the lunar low continues, this is probably not the best time during April in which to pursue new ideas. However, this needn't prevent you from making some progress, particularly at work. And for those Librans who work for themselves there could be the chance of a new and important contact today.

8 TUESDAY
Moon Age Day 2 Moon Sign Taurus

Joint financial matters are well accented, even if you have to draw in your horns a little regarding expenditure at home. It's possible you have been rather too lavish recently and if so the rest of this week offers an opportunity to look for savings in all possible directions. Never mind, things may be better than you think.

9 WEDNESDAY
Moon Age Day 3 Moon Sign Taurus

A sudden change of direction is possible, and trends suggest this is most likely at work. Maybe you will decide to take on something different, or could find yourself able to assume new responsibilities. Things may be rather less exciting at home, particularly if other people seem to be rather gloomy at the moment.

10 THURSDAY   *Moon Age Day 4 Moon Sign Gemini*

If you keep the current pace of activity quite brisk, you can remain at your most cheerful. This is in stark contrast to some of the people with whom you mix on a daily basis. Your attitude and actions will be infectious if you keep them up, and few people can avoid your happy smile today.

11 FRIDAY   *Moon Age Day 5 Moon Sign Gemini*

This would be a good period for taking the initiative. Others may think they have the answers but you will know for certain that you do. You can use all this confidence to get yourself noticed, and if it were possible you are also even chattier than usual at the moment. You can get on especially well with unusual types at present.

12 SATURDAY   *Moon Age Day 6 Moon Sign Cancer*

It shouldn't be hard to get into the good books of most people – to do so you don't need to do anything more complicated than being yourself. Of course you can't expect to be number one in everyone's books, and part of the reason for this may be jealousy. It ought to be possible to get a lot done in and around your home this weekend.

13 SUNDAY   *Moon Age Day 7 Moon Sign Cancer*

Keeping one eye on the progress made by family members and the other on any passing chance to have fun, you can make this a happy and generally carefree sort of Sunday. It could be even better if you are willing to get a few friends together and take some sort of trip – maybe to the coast or to a beautiful part of the country.

14 MONDAY   *Moon Age Day 8 Moon Sign Leo*

There are certain things that you know you have now outgrown – and we aren't talking about clothes here. The time is right for a sort-out and for coming to terms with the fact that situations and people sometimes change. New friendships can be started around now as you move one or two past associations into the background.

15 TUESDAY
Moon Age Day 9 Moon Sign Leo

Rather than bossing others around today, and you would be much better using gentle persuasion of the sort that Librans instinctively understand. Yours is the most diplomatic of all the zodiac signs and you do your best work when assessing how others are likely to react before you say anything at all.

16 WEDNESDAY
Moon Age Day 10 Moon Sign Virgo

A slower pace is encouraged whilst the Moon is in your solar twelfth house, and you probably won't get what you want today by acting like a bull in a china shop. Leave that sort of approach to others, whilst you show how far you can get with subtlety and guile. Ruthless types don't impress you at all at the moment.

17 THURSDAY
Moon Age Day 11 Moon Sign Virgo

Even if things are still quieter than you might wish, it shouldn't be long before that changes significantly. By tomorrow you can get right back into the mainstream of life, and that is why you can now get so much from a little prior planning. You may even choose to spend a few hours on your own and should enjoy the peace and quiet.

18 FRIDAY
Moon Age Day 12 Moon Sign Libra

You now enter a potentially much busier and more generally active period. The Moon occupies your zodiac sign and brings with it new incentives and a greater determination to get what you want from life in almost every way. A time to strengthen your finances and come up with new ideas for making additional cash.

19 SATURDAY
Moon Age Day 13 Moon Sign Libra

Don't be afraid to ask a few favours today. If you are charming in the way you approach others they are hardly likely to refuse any reasonable request. Even the odd extraordinary favour will be granted if you have the cheek to ask. Lady Luck is on your side and that makes this a time for taking a few chances.

20 SUNDAY
Moon Age Day 14 Moon Sign Libra

You can still get things working well for you in a general sense, though you needn't stick around in one place today in order to register the fact. You need fresh fields and pastures new, and the more the weather improves and the nights grow lighter, the greater will be your delight with life and your own abilities.

21 MONDAY
Moon Age Day 15 Moon Sign Scorpio

Any restlessness at the start of this week could be explained by the continuing power of the lunar high. Nothing that happens is fast enough for you and you may decide to force the pace from morning until night. Although you might get plenty done there is also a chance you will exhaust yourself on the way.

22 TUESDAY
Moon Age Day 16 Moon Sign Scorpio

Once again trends enhance your need for travel or at the very least a yearning to get away from the usual routines of the working week. Physical movement might not be possible for the moment, but that needn't prevent your mind from taking you anywhere you want to go. Fantasy is better than nothing at present.

23 WEDNESDAY
Moon Age Day 17 Moon Sign Sagittarius

The Moon is now in your solar third house, highlighting your ability to speak your mind in an emotional sense. Not that you ever need too much encouragement to tell people how you feel about them, but there can be something distinctly poetical to your approach now. New friends could now come good with promises.

24 THURSDAY
Moon Age Day 18 Moon Sign Sagittarius

Beware of getting involved in deep discussions today because with the passing of time these could turn into arguments – and that is something you hate. You strive all the time for a peaceful life and even though there are occasions when disputes cannot be avoided, for the moment at least you should manage to keep almost everyone sweet and happy.

25 FRIDAY · · · · · · · · · · *Moon Age Day 19 Moon Sign Sagittarius*

This is a good time to keep on the move, if only because others won't bother you too much if you don't stick around for long. You can easily get discouraged at the moment if colleagues or friends are negative in their attitudes. Better by far to continue with your own plans until they mature, rather than changing them now.

26 SATURDAY · · · · · · · · · · *Moon Age Day 20 Moon Sign Capricorn*

The Moon has now switched to your solar fourth house and that brings family matters into sharp relief. It could be that you feel guilty because you have not been spending as much time or attention on those you love, but this is probably an illusion as far as you are concerned. Libra can't help looking after everyone, and you are no exception.

27 SUNDAY · · · · · · · · · · *Moon Age Day 21 Moon Sign Capricorn*

Not everything is going to get done today, and if you realise the fact early in the day you shouldn't spend hours feeling guilty because something is being ignored. Do what is reasonable and avoid thinking of yourself as some sort of super-hero who has magical powers. Somewhere in the mix you need to consider your own weekend needs.

28 MONDAY · · · · · · · · · · *Moon Age Day 22 Moon Sign Aquarius*

This week could well start out with a few thorny issues in need of resolving. Any hold-ups and reversals come along to tell you that the time is right for rethinking your strategies. Some jobs may take longer than normal, but the important thing is to do everything to the best of your ability.

29 TUESDAY · · · · · · · · · · *Moon Age Day 23 Moon Sign Aquarius*

Trends encourage you to have your gaze firmly set upon the wider world, and great restlessness is possible if circumstances pin you to the same spot for more than a few hours. A day to keep up your efforts to revitalise your love life and also get involved with new social projects that are being suggested by friends. New financial incentives appear now.

30 WEDNESDAY   *Moon Age Day 24 Moon Sign Aquarius*

Play it safe in professional matters by taking the line of least resistance. You may not help yourself at the moment by being radical in your approach to anything, and Libra's usual calm and rational attitude definitely works best for you. There could be times today when you will need to repeat yourself three or four times in order to be heard.

May

2008

1 THURSDAY
Moon Age Day 25 Moon Sign Pisces

This is hardly the best time to be taking risks of any sort, and especially not where money is concerned. You can make May Day happy and carefree, just as long as you don't push yourself too hard. Why not take a walk in the garden or maybe in your local park and watch the flowers grow for a while? This is the sort of diversion that suits you.

2 FRIDAY
Moon Age Day 26 Moon Sign Pisces

Make the most of a short interlude of high-tension and lightning-quick reactions ahead of the lunar low. If there is anything that really needs to be done, get it out of the way today and then settle back for a couple of days during which you can recharge flagging batteries. It's worth planning now for a weekend of leisure and relaxation.

3 SATURDAY
Moon Age Day 27 Moon Sign Aries

This is hardly the best time of the month to be taking risks of any kind, and especially not when it comes to cash. Fortunately there is a great deal of truth in the adage that the best things in life are free. Nobody can put a value on love or personal ties, and you can afford to find the time necessary to spend with those you care for.

4 SUNDAY
Moon Age Day 28 Moon Sign Aries

You need to do what seems right to you at the moment, even if this means withdrawing into yourself a great deal more than would normally be the case. Progress continues to be slow, but there is nothing at all wrong with that. There are ways and means to stand up for yourself and your point of view today, though without undue argument.

5 MONDAY
Moon Age Day 0 Moon Sign Taurus

Now you can benefit from widening your horizons and from looking at all sorts of new possibilities, some of which might have been staring you in the face for a while now. Your best approach is to set your sights firmly on the future and don't allow nostalgia or misplaced sentiment to get in your way under present planetary trends.

6 TUESDAY
Moon Age Day 1 Moon Sign Taurus

If you put your point of view across rather too strongly today, you could give offence when none was intended. This is unusual for diplomatic Libra, and is supported by the position of Mars in your solar chart at present. Part of the situation could also be down to a little frustration with others.

7 WEDNESDAY
Moon Age Day 2 Moon Sign Gemini

This has got to be a very good time for getting your professional life moving positively and for making decisions that are going to have a bearing on your life for some time to come. Trends assist you to be definite, confident and desirous of change. The only slight fly in the ointment comes from trying to alter too much all at once.

8 THURSDAY
Moon Age Day 3 Moon Sign Gemini

A day to keep in touch with groups of like-minded individuals and don't forget that you need to stimulate the more intellectual side of your nature, as well as concentrating on your work. You will soon get both bored and dull if you don't have interests coming in from alternative directions. Libra is up for new hobbies this month.

9 FRIDAY
Moon Age Day 4 Moon Sign Cancer

You can allow your sense of personal freedom to grow day by day, and that means you can break out of those moulds you now find to be too restricting. Trust Libra to do the unexpected, just when everyone thinks they have you taped. But it's this side of your nature that keeps the world guessing and which makes you so fascinating.

10 SATURDAY   *Moon Age Day 5 Moon Sign Cancer*

Long-distance travel and communications with people from far and near are highlighted at the moment. With the weekend comes an opportunity to see something completely new – though the object or place itself could be extremely old. What matters is that you don't spend all day staring at what you already know.

11 SUNDAY   *Moon Age Day 6 Moon Sign Leo*

Confidence to do the right thing remains extremely strong, and you may decide to shock a few people! Libra isn't usually meant to be this way but you are, after all, born of an Air sign and this makes you unpredictable on occasions. Your usual gentleness of nature is sometimes replaced by fire and turbulent emotions.

12 MONDAY   *Moon Age Day 7 Moon Sign Leo*

As a new week gets started you have a chance to settle down somewhat and be more like your usual self, especially where work is concerned. However, there are still bursts of electricity coming from you and you can use these to attract your share of admirers whilst you continue to shock people!

13 TUESDAY   *Moon Age Day 8 Moon Sign Virgo*

A quieter time is possible, and for this you can thank a twelfth-house Moon. Not that this makes much difference in terms of the way the world views you at present. Now, instead of pushing energy out in every conceivable direction you should be simmering slowly – which probably makes you even more fascinating than before.

14 WEDNESDAY   *Moon Age Day 9 Moon Sign Virgo*

It's worth getting any jobs out of the way that demand your sole attention. You should be quite happy to spend time on your own and won't need the constant stimulation that comes from being part of a group. Even where your social life is concerned you may be now more amenable to solo pursuits – even if friends demand your attention.

15 THURSDAY   *Moon Age Day 10 Moon Sign Virgo*

Trends support a real desire for creature comforts, and you might be more than happy to spend fairly long periods doing whatever takes your fancy, though in a solitary and insular sort of way. This is a very temporary interlude because by tomorrow everything changes yet again. Keeping up with your moods now isn't easy.

16 FRIDAY   *Moon Age Day 11 Moon Sign Libra*

With the lunar high comes a chance to break the bounds of the possible and to make as many contacts with the wider world as you can. You probably won't take at all kindly to being pigeon-holed or restricted in any way, and should be doing all you can to show just how original you truly are. This is a great time to start a new romance.

17 SATURDAY   *Moon Age Day 12 Moon Sign Libra*

Lady Luck is waiting in the wings to pay you more than one visit during the next twenty-four hours. This does not mean that you should take chances or expect too much of any sort of speculation. Use your intuition but also latch onto the power that comes from being able to put yourself in the right place at the best possible time.

18 SUNDAY   *Moon Age Day 13 Moon Sign Scorpio*

Even if you feel ready to handle a variety of interests right now, there may be people around who seem determined to hold you back in some way. It's difficult, because some individuals probably do have your best interests at heart, whilst others may be envious or even jealous. Sorting out the wheat from the chaff is not easy.

19 MONDAY   *Moon Age Day 14 Moon Sign Scorpio*

You continue to make gains from having something new and interesting on which to focus your attention. For a day or two your powers of discrimination are not at their best, so medium- or long-term decision-making is not to be recommended. It would be better by far to wait and see, whilst also listening to some sound advice.

20 TUESDAY　　　*Moon Age Day 15　Moon Sign Scorpio*

Aspects of love are all around you – coming both from family members and from a romantic direction. With all the emotional demands that are being made upon you, it may not be at all easy to decide who you ought to be with next. Your best approach is to compartmentalise your day and be very strict in how you allot your time.

21 WEDNESDAY　　*Moon Age Day 16　Moon Sign Sagittarius*

Life gets ever more interesting, though with Venus now in your solar eighth house this may be a period to think about some fairly widespread changes in the way you deal with your emotional life. For some Librans the time has come to make a change, or at least to alter the emphasis of a relationship that is now growing tired or stale.

22 THURSDAY　　*Moon Age Day 17　Moon Sign Sagittarius*

There are signs that someone out there is now only too willing to help you achieve a longed-for objective, and this may be the one person you never thought of as being on your side. It only goes to prove that you can't know everything, and that even when you think you have people taped, they turn out to be quite different.

23 FRIDAY　　　*Moon Age Day 18　Moon Sign Capricorn*

You can afford to make enjoyment your number one priority right now, and even if you are still busy in a practical sense, you should also appreciate that all work and no play is going to make you duller and less interesting. Social arrangements are down to you, both now and for the weekend ahead, so you need to get your thinking cap on.

24 SATURDAY　　*Moon Age Day 19　Moon Sign Capricorn*

The weekend responds best if you avoid arguments or disputes within the family and spend time with friends instead of relatives. You can contribute to discussions, but not if everyone wants to speak at the same time and refuses to modify their own point of view. What you really want today is peace and quiet.

25 SUNDAY   *Moon Age Day 20 Moon Sign Capricorn*

Venus has now moved into your solar ninth house. This helps you to make life more interesting and assists you when it comes to enlarging your scope and broadening your horizons generally. Small details should be easier to address, and you have what it takes to concentrate on something very tiny and yet immensely important.

26 MONDAY   *Moon Age Day 21 Moon Sign Aquarius*

A new week begins and you can discover a better clarity when it comes to addressing career issues and the part you play in determining your own future. If you aren't happy for others to make up their minds on your behalf, don't be afraid to fight like a tiger to have your own say – even when it isn't remotely important to do so.

27 TUESDAY   ☿ *Moon Age Day 22 Moon Sign Aquarius*

Bringing out the best in others is a natural gift to Libra and one you rarely abandon for more than a day or two at a time. In this respect you should now be definitely back to normal, and can make yourself easier for others to understand. A particular job might appear to take a long time today but it is worth pursuing to its conclusion.

28 WEDNESDAY ☿   *Moon Age Day 23 Moon Sign Pisces*

You have what it takes to get most issues running smoothly in the middle of the week and to show yourself functioning well if others are watching you closely. You won't always be aware that you are under scrutiny, but it's worth assuming that you are in the spotlight for most of the day. By the evening you can afford some relaxation.

29 THURSDAY   ☿ *Moon Age Day 24 Moon Sign Pisces*

Standard responses won't work all that well at present, which is why your originality proves to be of such importance at the moment. You can be a delight to have around and can make sure others enjoy your company, either at work or socially. Today might not prove to be remarkable, but it can be both satisfying and enjoyable.

30 FRIDAY ☿ *Moon Age Day 25 Moon Sign Aries*

Why not just go with the flow today? You can't make things happen in quite the way you would wish and the lunar low encourages you to look on the black side of some situations. There isn't much point in acting on impulse under present trends, because whichever way you choose to jump could well be the wrong way!

31 SATURDAY ☿ *Moon Age Day 26 Moon Sign Aries*

Your strengths are best saved for a different time. You can afford to let others make most of the decisions at present and to be willing to follow their lead. Of course this applies to individuals you know and trust and not to strangers who may not have your best interests at heart. Don't worry if you feel fatigued today – it shouldn't last long.

June

2008

1 SUNDAY ☿ *Moon Age Day 27 Moon Sign Taurus*

Sunday the first of June offers a rapid change to circumstances and the way you feel about them. You can make great gains through any form of travel and might decide to undertake a journey that has only been arranged at the last minute. The summer has now well and truly arrived, so make the most of it.

2 MONDAY ☿ *Moon Age Day 28 Moon Sign Taurus*

There could well be a battle of wills going on at the moment, with you right in the middle of it. Although you are generally easy-going and willing to fall in line with the status quo, this is probably not the case right now. Your attitude might shock someone, but it is not a bad thing to shake people up once in a while!

3 TUESDAY ☿ *Moon Age Day 29 Moon Sign Gemini*

You need to put yourself in the most advantageous position today, especially at work, and particularly so if you are involved in any form of education at present. The way you come across to others is extremely important, and you shouldn't stay at the back of any class sitting on your hands. Don't follow today, but lead!

4 WEDNESDAY ☿ *Moon Age Day 0 Moon Sign Gemini*

The time is right to strike, and this applies to just about any facet of your life. Even if things are quieter in a personal sense, you can show your best side to the world at large. Your capabilities have never been so pronounced as they are right now, and you can persuade others to take your ideas and plans into account.

5 THURSDAY ☿ *Moon Age Day 1 Moon Sign Cancer*

Group matters are now favourably highlighted, assisting you to perform very well when you are at the head of a team, or at least contributing significantly to it. This could also be a day of presents, when gifts can be obtained from some quite unusual directions. Something you did in the past could now be revisiting you fortunately.

6 FRIDAY ☿ *Moon Age Day 2 Moon Sign Cancer*

Your enthusiasm continues unabated, which should make you good to have around. Libra is a delightful zodiac sign because you are able to compliment others, whilst at the same time displaying sincerity and integrity. You can use today to strengthen relationships, especially new ones.

7 SATURDAY ☿ *Moon Age Day 3 Moon Sign Leo*

Some objectives now need abandoning for good, if only because you can't do everything you would wish. You will discover this weekend that it is better to do one thing properly than to be half-baked about a number of options. If it proves to be necessary, be prepared to seek out the help and advice of an expert.

8 SUNDAY ☿ *Moon Age Day 4 Moon Sign Leo*

You have what it takes to attract all the support you need this Sunday, though if leisure and pleasure are more important to you at the moment than advancement, you may not be too keen to get involved in very practical or professional issues. Libra needs to relax, and there are any number of options open to you on this June day.

9 MONDAY ☿ *Moon Age Day 5 Moon Sign Leo*

Trends encourage you to seek out people who can broaden your perspectives, particularly in a work sense. You should also get out to places you haven't explored before, because this too can offer you an altered perspective. Anything that makes you think more expansively is good.

10 TUESDAY ☿ *Moon Age Day 6 Moon Sign Virgo*

There could be a slight emphasis today on personal concerns and probably also on family members, some of whom are behaving in a fairly unusual way. You can use your usual Libran tact to find out what is going on, and do everything you can to put matters right. This should be possible under present trends.

11 WEDNESDAY ☿ *Moon Age Day 7 Moon Sign Virgo*

Make the most of a slight reprieve from everyday concerns and worries by going deep inside your own mind for much of today. It isn't that you are feeling unsociable, merely that you have the chance to think things through. Bearing in mind that the lunar high is imminent, a little forward planning could turn out to be very sensible.

12 THURSDAY ☿ *Moon Age Day 8 Moon Sign Libra*

Use the energy that surrounds you for the next two days both to increase your luck and to push forward the bounds of the possible. You should be in a position to meet a few very interesting people today, and some of them could prove to be useful to you both now and in the months ahead. Your own popularity is well accented.

13 FRIDAY ☿ *Moon Age Day 9 Moon Sign Libra*

The lunar high offers another favourable day for getting what you want and for making arrangements at more or less the last minute. Others should admire your brinkmanship, and even if this way of going on doesn't suit you as a rule, you manage very well for now. It is your spontaneity that gets you most noticed in company today.

14 SATURDAY ☿ *Moon Age Day 10 Moon Sign Scorpio*

Don't be afraid to keep up your present search for change and variety. With Venus in your solar ninth house you can also seek new intellectual experiences. Even if not everyone around you understands the way your mind is working for the moment, that doesn't matter because you also have what it takes to charm the birds from the trees.

15 SUNDAY ☿ *Moon Age Day 11 Moon Sign Scorpio*

A combination of excitement and restlessness is on offer now that you have so many ninth-house planets. The Sun is also there, and all things considered you would be better off not making any cast-iron arrangements for socialising today. Keep it light and flexible, and you can make just about anything happen!

16 MONDAY ☿ *Moon Age Day 12 Moon Sign Scorpio*

The signs are that your ideas and opinions may not appeal to everyone at the start of this new working week. This could be especially true in a professional sense. Your best approach is to explain yourself very carefully and to give those around you the chance to air their views as well. You can get your own way if you at least appear flexible.

17 TUESDAY ☿ *Moon Age Day 13 Moon Sign Sagittarius*

Be prepared to communicate what you feel to just about anyone who will listen today. Your mind is complex and some of what you propose may not be easy for others to understand. The more time you take to make your notions clear to those around you, the greater will be you own comprehension of the way you feel.

18 WEDNESDAY ☿ *Moon Age Day 14 Moon Sign Sagittarius*

Today offers a refreshing and inspiring social scene, and people who come new to your life at this time could well become deep and abiding friends eventually. When it comes to getting changes underway at home you would be best off looking at original possibilities. An ideal time to brighten up your castle.

19 THURSDAY ☿ *Moon Age Day 15 Moon Sign Capricorn*

If many of your emotions are quite close to the surface today, you could find yourself to be in a very sentimental frame of mind. Part of this is brought about by nostalgia and by thinking deeply about long-past situations. All of this is fine just as long as you realise that you live in the present, which has its own different needs.

20 FRIDAY
☿ *Moon Age Day 16   Moon Sign Capricorn*

By all means seek stimulation from new people, though you also need to bear old friends in mind. Even if they seem less than inspiring right now, when the chips are down you can always rely on them. Romance is in the air for some Librans under present trends, and you have scope to bring passion to new relationships.

21 SATURDAY
Moon Age Day 17   Moon Sign Capricorn

You are now deep into a phase during which enjoying personal freedoms and broadening your horizons in a general sense should be very much easier. Travel is well starred, and those Librans who have chosen this period to take a holiday were certainly inspired. Even a short trip could help you no end.

22 SUNDAY
Moon Age Day 18   Moon Sign Aquarius

It's time to make a difference. If you aren't working on a Sunday, you can afford to turn your attention to socialising and also to improving your personal environment in some way. If the weather is really good you might decide on a barbeque or some other sort of party that gets everyone involved.

23 MONDAY
Moon Age Day 19   Moon Sign Aquarius

Your strength lies in refusing to be kept down today and in expressing your views at every possible opportunity. This can be achieved without anyone feeling threatened, because you have what it takes to put across even the most radical ideas in a way that appeals to colleagues and friends.

24 TUESDAY
Moon Age Day 20   Moon Sign Pisces

In the main what you get out of life today is directly proportional to the amount of effort you put in. Rather than being too quick to jump to any conclusions, it's worth working steadily towards your objectives, bearing in mind that you only have one pair of hands. A calm and rational approach will help you to gain rewards.

25 WEDNESDAY   *Moon Age Day 21 Moon Sign Pisces*

Major opportunities for advancement are now available, and these lie mainly in professional matters. Librans who are involved in full-time education may be in the best possible position to achieve successes, and all of you can make sense of something that was only recently a deep mystery.

26 THURSDAY   *Moon Age Day 22 Moon Sign Pisces*

A couple of quieter days are now possible, so it is quite important to get those very urgent jobs out of the way right now. Although you may find the real assistance you need to be slightly lacking today, you can still bamboozle others into lending a hand, even if you have to baffle them with science. Your charm can work wonders!

27 FRIDAY   *Moon Age Day 23 Moon Sign Aries*

Energy and enthusiasm are not emphasised by the lunar low and between now and Sunday you may have to rely quite heavily on the good offices of relatives and friends in order to get what you want from life. This may not go down easily after such a long period of self-choices and personally inspired decisions.

28 SATURDAY   *Moon Age Day 24 Moon Sign Aries*

Don't be afraid to sit on the fence today. In any case nobody does it better than you. Don't allow yourself to be forced into situations that mean you making long-term decisions, because present trends don't assist you to see ahead of yourself as much as you would wish. Why not accept some support today?

29 SUNDAY   *Moon Age Day 25 Moon Sign Taurus*

On a social level you can now make life quite interesting and since the less favourable aspects of the lunar low are now out of the way you can be far more progressive and better able to make important decisions. What a difference a day makes, and how happy you should feel to be alive and to move around freely.

30 MONDAY

Moon Age Day 26 Moon Sign Taurus

This is a time during which you have scope to capitalise on the opportunity to do something novel or different. The more variety you manage to get into your life, the better you are likely to feel. Ring the changes all through the day and get some fresh air at some stage. Even a walk in the park would be better than nothing.

July

2008

1 TUESDAY   *Moon Age Day 27 Moon Sign Gemini*

It is professional interests that matter the most on the first day of July, whilst those Librans who are between jobs at the moment would be wise to keep their eyes open for any new possibilities that are around. Energy levels remain high, and now that the Sun is in your solar tenth house you can capitalise much more on new starts.

2 WEDNESDAY   *Moon Age Day 28 Moon Sign Gemini*

Some hopeful or interesting news is now available, on a day during which communications of all sorts prove to be especially important. The time is right to make sure you keep up contact with others, even if this means gossiping!

3 THURSDAY   *Moon Age Day 0 Moon Sign Cancer*

It is towards the unusual or the downright odd that your mind is now encouraged to turn. You shouldn't be at all put out by having to change horses in midstream, either at work or home, and true to your Air-sign heritage you can remain flexible in every area of your life. It's worth keeping up your efforts to bring others out of their self-imposed shell.

4 FRIDAY   *Moon Age Day 1 Moon Sign Cancer*

Now is the part of the year to put yourself in the best company, and a period that responds best to maximum effort in a social sense. Not everyone wants to be your friend, but that's life, and you can't make people like you. Instead of worrying about this, concentrate on those individuals who clearly think you are fascinating and sexy.

114

5 SATURDAY *Moon Age Day 2 Moon Sign Leo*

Charm and flattery work well for you this weekend and particularly so if you are dealing with people you have found to be rather awkward in the past. This is a good day for shopping and for seeking out a very special bargain. Routines may not look very appealing today.

6 SUNDAY *Moon Age Day 3 Moon Sign Leo*

If there is one commodity that you really need right now it is discipline. This is just as important when you are dealing with domestic matters as it is when you are at work. In particular you might have decided that the time is right for a spring-clean, but this won't be of much use if you refuse to throw away anything at all. Don't be afraid to be ruthless.

7 MONDAY *Moon Age Day 4 Moon Sign Virgo*

A potentially quieter day, and one that isn't ideal for addressing practical matters. This is a time to take stock and a day when you would be better off letting others do most of the work. Even if you are not feeling lazy, the position of the Moon conspires against your energy levels.

8 TUESDAY *Moon Age Day 5 Moon Sign Virgo*

That twelfth-house Moon is still around, and although you can get a great deal of enjoyment out of today, you may not be at your best in terms of physical achievements. However, a professional matter offers you scope to move into a fairly dominant role, and even if you tire easily in a muscular sense, there's nothing wrong with your brain.

9 WEDNESDAY *Moon Age Day 6 Moon Sign Libra*

Now your energies are highlighted and you can really let the sap rise. What has been merely mental effort across the last couple of days finds physical manifestations. You might be on a one-person campaign to sort out the neighbourhood in which you live, and you will certainly be well equipped to achieve a high degree of success at work.

10 THURSDAY   *Moon Age Day 7 Moon Sign Libra*

The continuing lunar high favours new interests, and you have everything it takes to make the best impression on the world that has been possible so far this year. Almost everything you do is calculated to impress those around you, and even when you have no intention of attracting attention, it happens anyway. You can't help shining!

11 FRIDAY   *Moon Age Day 8 Moon Sign Libra*

It isn't the destination you achieve today that matters but rather the means by which you get there. This is just as important in terms of your thinking as it would be regarding any physical journey. You have what it takes to do things right and will be particularly powerful in your ability to sort out the problems of others.

12 SATURDAY   *Moon Age Day 9 Moon Sign Scorpio*

With Mars now in your solar twelfth house, certain parts of your life could seem like a drag. There is really only one way to deal with this situation and that is to pitch in anyway. You should soon discover that the means you use to get jobs done become fascinating in their own right, and you can turn a chore into a pleasure.

13 SUNDAY   *Moon Age Day 10 Moon Sign Scorpio*

If you are a weekend worker, trends assist you to get on extremely well in a professional sense, and you may well find that you are being relied on much more than you might have expected. This is especially true if you have only just started a new job. For relaxing Librans there should be a chance to spruce up your house or garden.

14 MONDAY   *Moon Age Day 11 Moon Sign Sagittarius*

This has potential to be a day of hectic comings and goings, both by yourself and almost everyone with whom you make contact. It's hard to maintain control of some situations, and keeping people on track may be quite difficult too. Your best approach is to keep an open mind and smile whenever you can.

15 TUESDAY   *Moon Age Day 12 Moon Sign Sagittarius*

You benefit from showing a very light touch in debates and discussions, whilst still being able to get your point of view across quite forcefully. You might even surprise yourself with your mental agility, but this will not be a puzzle to those who know you the best. Trends offer you scope for advances of a romantic sort.

16 WEDNESDAY   *Moon Age Day 13 Moon Sign Sagittarius*

Group encounters and places of interest and entertainment are a must today if you want to get the very best from what is on offer in a planetary sense. Don't let yourself be pigeonholed, and make sure everyone knows you are around, even if you have to do something startling to prove the fact. A day to enjoy funny incidents.

17 THURSDAY   *Moon Age Day 14 Moon Sign Capricorn*

You have potential to be very productive at the moment, and can turn your fertile mind in just about any direction. It may not always be the easiest course of action that seems most appealing to you, but getting there in the end is within your grasp. The only slight difficulty could be bringing others round to your point of view.

18 FRIDAY   *Moon Age Day 15 Moon Sign Capricorn*

If trifling matters and social obligations keep you on the go this Friday, you could end the day feeling tired but satisfied. From a social point of view you have everything to play for and should be quite ready to join in when it comes to painting the town red. However, bearing in mind the exhaustion, a pale pink may be more likely!

19 SATURDAY   *Moon Age Day 16 Moon Sign Aquarius*

The most important aspect today comes about as a result of the position of the Moon in your solar chart. This puts the focus on romance, so be prepared to play the Romeo or Juliet. Fortunately you shouldn't have to go through the trials and tribulations that attended that particular couple.

20 SUNDAY   *Moon Age Day 17 Moon Sign Aquarius*

When it comes to being in the know you won't be left out today, and so may decide to dig and delve into every recess of life. This allows you to make discoveries you never suspected, but could also bring you to a realisation that may be less than fortunate. Confidence remains strong, as does your general physical state.

21 MONDAY   *Moon Age Day 18 Moon Sign Aquarius*

Certain duties could now prove to be a real test of your patience and so it is fortunate that you have plenty. Today responds best if you keep trying until you achieve your desired objectives. Even if colleagues and friends fall by the wayside, you shouldn't allow yourself to be beaten and can come up trumps.

22 TUESDAY   *Moon Age Day 19 Moon Sign Pisces*

Friends may be particularly important to you at this time and could play a great part in your thinking. Trends encourage you to look again at acquaintances, and maybe turn them into trusted friends. Take the time to show your appreciation to a loved one at some stage today.

23 WEDNESDAY   *Moon Age Day 20 Moon Sign Pisces*

With a great deal of affection at the moment, both coming to you and from you, you can make this a warm and happy sort of day. You might not be quite as go-getting as has been the case recently and especially not later in the day. It's worth finishing one job before you start the next, and preparing yourself for a quieter and less dynamic period.

24 THURSDAY   *Moon Age Day 21 Moon Sign Aries*

The lunar low encourages a focus on minor duties and responsibilities, and you may not have a great deal of extra energy to plough into your social life. Libra can afford to choose a comfortable armchair whenever possible and simply vegetate in front of the television. Don't worry, this phase won't last long.

25 FRIDAY
Moon Age Day 22 Moon Sign Aries

Be prepared to wind down your activities, though explaining to others why you have suddenly put on the brakes won't be too easy. What makes matters even more difficult is that you can get right back in there again tomorrow. Never mind, it does no real harm to keep people guessing sometimes – it increases your mystique!

26 SATURDAY
Moon Age Day 23 Moon Sign Taurus

It appears that the focus today is on the grass roots of your life and it could be the most basic matters that tend to occupy your mind. Speaking of grass roots, you might decide to mow the lawn or weed a flowerbed. Such tasks, though often quite a chore, could appeal to you under present planetary trends. Why not find time to support loved ones?

27 SUNDAY
Moon Age Day 24 Moon Sign Taurus

There are signs that casual contacts will mean as much to you today as the most important relationships, particularly if acquaintances are being mysterious or attentive. You will be on good social form and have scope to ring the changes as much as possible. Librans who have opted for a holiday at this time have certainly chosen well.

28 MONDAY
Moon Age Day 25 Moon Sign Gemini

Do keep your life as interesting and varied as you can. You never know what exciting highways and byways are there for your discovery. Even if there are interruptions to your general routines, you can take these very much in your stride. You can afford to have confidence in a project that is now doing well.

29 TUESDAY
Moon Age Day 26 Moon Sign Gemini

Venus, now in your solar eleventh house, assists you to move into the public eye. It is possible that others are putting you firmly on a pedestal. That's fine as far as it goes but you know only too well that this can mean there is a long way to fall. Don't worry, your sense of social balance is very good.

30 WEDNESDAY   *Moon Age Day 27 Moon Sign Cancer*

Be on the lookout for social newcomers and recognise that this is not the best time to be standing still. On the contrary, the more effort you put into life, the greater can be the rewards. A day to firm up arrangements for travel, and to check carefully any sort of document you have to sign.

31 THURSDAY   *Moon Age Day 28 Moon Sign Cancer*

Some accomplishments are still possible, even if you feel as though you are faltering a little. You have what it takes to attract a good deal of natural help from life itself, and although this is certainly not the right time to be gambling, the odd very calculated risk might be worthwhile. Consult your intuition, which is strong now.

August

2008

1 FRIDAY
Moon Age Day 0 Moon Sign Leo

Whilst Mars remains in your solar twelfth house it might be sensible to avoid busy schedules for now if you can. Taking on too many demands might mean that only half the things you want to achieve are completed to your satisfaction. The last thing you want at the moment is to get frustrated with yourself.

2 SATURDAY
Moon Age Day 1 Moon Sign Leo

Today resonds best if you try to avoid anyone you consider to be vulgar or irritating. This could include neighbours, casual social contacts or colleagues. Stick to those individuals you have know for quite a while and be prepared to remove yourself from situations that bother you.

3 SUNDAY
Moon Age Day 2 Moon Sign Virgo

Right now you do need good, solid friendships in order to be at your happiest. The problem is that these associations come at a price, because it appears that everyone had some sort of demand to make of you. As a rule you show great patience when dealing with others, but even Libra can't be sweetness and light all the time.

4 MONDAY
Moon Age Day 3 Moon Sign Virgo

You will probably enjoy being around other people today and can get a great deal from groups of almost any sort. Rather than spending too much time on its own at the moment, Libra can show itself to be very gregarious. Just be careful you don't end up cracking jokes that turn out to be somewhat less than appropriate.

5 TUESDAY
Moon Age Day 4 Moon Sign Virgo

Even if you are not quite as outgoing today as was the case yesterday, you can still make people laugh and should be quite happy to jog along with others. A little isolation later in the day might be in order. This will be a chance to think through some of those ingenious ideas that are coursing around in your head at the moment.

6 WEDNESDAY
Moon Age Day 5 Moon Sign Libra

The lunar high encourages you to seek help from the most unlikely of directions today, even before you even needed it. This can be a crackerjack of a day but you do need to react quickly to changing circumstances and to take your chances when they appear. There is absolutely no time for modesty or for hiding your light under a bushel.

7 THURSDAY
Moon Age Day 6 Moon Sign Libra

When it comes to getting others to adopt your ideas, you have potential to be the master at the moment. You can persuade almost anyone to fall before your charm and listen to your sound common sense. You can afford to back your hunches more than you normally would, and can show great courage when it is necessary.

8 FRIDAY
Moon Age Day 7 Moon Sign Scorpio

It is social trends that really shine out today, offering you scope to mix freely with the greatest cross-section of individuals you can. The focus is on compromise, and even on those occasions when you cannot accept the plans that colleagues or friends are putting forward, you can suggest acceptable alternatives.

9 SATURDAY
Moon Age Day 8 Moon Sign Scorpio

There could be distinct benefits from making time to be on your own at some stage today. Venus is now in your solar twelfth house, and this does encourage you to be rather reflective, particularly where personal attachments are concerned. When you emerge from your little cocoon, it may well be to help a friend.

10 SUNDAY   *Moon Age Day 9 Moon Sign Sagittarius*

As a direct contrast to yesterday the emphasis now is back on communication and the need you have to be in good company. Be prepared to put your energy into absorbing the information you simply must have. Not all of this is imbibed for purely practical reasons, and there is a great sense of fun on offer now.

11 MONDAY   *Moon Age Day 10 Moon Sign Sagittarius*

Right now you have excellent instincts for teamwork and for getting jobs right in conjunction with colleagues. Libran individuals who work on their own or who are between jobs or retired may decide to forge different sorts of alliances at present. You are far from being a solitary creature at present and should relish company.

12 TUESDAY   *Moon Age Day 11 Moon Sign Sagittarius*

At home you have what it takes to be a good diplomat and to absorb any criticism that is coming from your partner or family members. If you realise that this is not directed specifically at you, you can pour oil on troubled waters. In most situations now you can be calm and collected.

13 WEDNESDAY   *Moon Age Day 12 Moon Sign Capricorn*

There may well be situations around today that will test your patience, but fortunately these are likely to be few and far between. What might upset you just a little is being around people who seem to do the wrong thing time and again, no matter how much you advise them to the contrary. Even your tolerance has its limits.

14 THURSDAY   *Moon Age Day 13 Moon Sign Capricorn*

Don't let others misunderstand you, even if it means explaining yourself time and again. Positive thinking might not be your forte at present, and you may need significant proof before you would embark on anything you see as being chancy or potentially hazardous. You might even decide to stick to rules for most of today

15 FRIDAY   *Moon Age Day 14 Moon Sign Aquarius*

There is yet more enjoyment to be had from relationships, and particularly from romantic attachments. If the love of your life needs a little pepping up, now is the time to put in that extra bit of effort. You could be very surprised by the result, and by the level of popularity you can achieve with your lover.

16 SATURDAY   *Moon Age Day 15 Moon Sign Aquarius*

It's possible that obstacles might arise at the moment that you cannot get through or round. Instead of bemoaning the fact it would be best to stand back and rethink your strategy. There is absolutely no point in banging your head against a wall, and everything suggests that if you spend time thinking about it, there is always another way.

17 SUNDAY   *Moon Age Day 16 Moon Sign Aquarius*

Keep a careful focus on objectives and make sure that you are well organised from the very start of today. It's true that now is not the best time of the month for innovations, and you act best when you know what is expected of you. This might all make for a slightly lacklustre sort of Sunday were it not for the input you can gain from friends.

18 MONDAY   *Moon Age Day 17 Moon Sign Pisces*

Career issues are not favoured by the present position of the Moon. In order to counteract a slight unfortunate trend you need to be well prepared and to plan anything you have to say to colleagues or superiors well in advance. Even then, extra care would be wise in order to avoid gaffes.

19 TUESDAY   *Moon Age Day 18 Moon Sign Pisces*

This is not an ideal time to try to dominate in relationships. This doesn't mean that you have to capitulate entirely and do everything that others suggest you should. Your best approach is simply to avoid issues you don't like the look of and to put off decisions until a slightly later date.

20 WEDNESDAY   *Moon Age Day 19 Moon Sign Aries*

You may simply have to make the best of a slightly bad lot whilst the lunar low is around. Paradoxically you won't necessarily be unhappy with life just now, and should easily be able to see the funny side of any situations that go somewhat askew. Personal attachments are favoured, despite the presence of the lunar low today and tomorrow.

21 THURSDAY   *Moon Age Day 20 Moon Sign Aries*

If this seems like a low point in your fortunes, thank your lucky stars that you can get back on course by tomorrow. The secret is not to let anything be taken too seriously and also not to give in over any issue you see as being important. Don't be afraid to rest and retrench because in a day or two your success rate could be very much higher.

22 FRIDAY   *Moon Age Day 21 Moon Sign Taurus*

Mars is now in your solar first house, bringing the start of a much more progressive period and allowing you to cope extremely well with nearly all practical situations. You can find new outlets for all the energy that is coursing through your veins, and needn't take no for an answer once you have made up your mind to any course of action.

23 SATURDAY   *Moon Age Day 22 Moon Sign Taurus*

The past could well have a great influence over you for a day or two, and this can be either a good or a bad thing. Being nostalgic for its own sake isn't going to help you at all, but learning from past mistakes can be. Attitude is very important if you are dealing with people you have found slightly difficult to face on previous occasions.

24 SUNDAY   *Moon Age Day 23 Moon Sign Gemini*

Right now you need great trust, good company and excellent ideas for the future. Keep up a sense of optimism and you can't go far wrong, though there could be moments today when you doubt your own capabilities for a while. One thing is certain, you can get yourself tuned in to what motivates other people.

25 MONDAY
Moon Age Day 24 Moon Sign Gemini

Now is the time to show yourself to be truly independent, and although this might not go down well with everyone, you do need to make up your own mind about almost everything and won't take kindly to being told what you should do. Beware of arguments though, because rows rarely help you in any way.

26 TUESDAY
Moon Age Day 25 Moon Sign Gemini

Venus remains in your solar twelfth house, which can be slightly problematic in relationships, especially when set against your present first-house Mars. Even if you want to be progressive when dealing with love, someone close to you may well be dragging their feet. What is the way forward? Your usual Libran patience.

27 WEDNESDAY
Moon Age Day 26 Moon Sign Cancer

Trends now encourage an even greater desire to help others all you can. There's nothing particularly unusual about this, except in terms of degree. You might need to be a little careful, because some of the advice and practical assistance you are offering may not be wanted and probably won't be welcomed by everyone.

28 THURSDAY
Moon Age Day 27 Moon Sign Cancer

In addition to Venus, Mercury is now temporarily in your solar twelfth house and for a while this offers scope for a somewhat quieter time than usual. A silent Libran is so unusual that someone is sure to think you are off colour or else worrying about something. Try to explain that you are fine and simply having a quiet interlude.

29 FRIDAY
Moon Age Day 28 Moon Sign Leo

A degree of social reluctance is possible, and you may decide to spend time on your own or with loved ones, rather than throwing in your lot with party animals. You can regain your usual joie de vivre before very long, so for the moment why not simply revel in the chance to be alone with your thoughts?

30 SATURDAY   *Moon Age Day 29 Moon Sign Leo*

Hooray! Mercury has now moved into your solar first house, which means it is in Libra. This assists you to come out of yourself in an instant and show that happy-go-lucky attitude that everyone loves best. You would be wise to keep your eyes and ears open today because there are things happening that should interest you.

31 SUNDAY   *Moon Age Day 0 Moon Sign Virgo*

Just when things began to get interesting the Moon moves into your solar twelfth house, once again offering a quieter and more contemplative interlude. This creates a sort of seesaw situation that others might find slightly difficult to understand. From their perspective you may be happy and cheerful one moment and almost silent the next!

September

2008

1 MONDAY
Moon Age Day 1   Moon Sign Virgo

The first of September offers you the opportunity to sort out a few details, and even if you are quiet your powers of reasoning could be particularly good. By tomorrow everything will change once more and so this would be an excellent time to plan ahead. Be prepared to get ever more progressive as the week wears on.

2 TUESDAY
Moon Age Day 2   Moon Sign Libra

Make this a period of initiative and self-reliance. You can achieve some fairly easy successes and shouldn't have to rely on the good offices of others in order to get ahead in almost any way. Lady Luck could well be on your side in financial matters, and a very limited form of speculation would be no bad thing.

3 WEDNESDAY
Moon Age Day 3   Moon Sign Libra

The potential for real success remains in place and you can make a great deal of headway with plans that have lain dormant for quite some time. Nor do you have to struggle on by yourself because you are not lacking in your usual ability to get others on board. Such is your popularity that you can persuade almost anyone to help you out.

4 THURSDAY
Moon Age Day 4   Moon Sign Scorpio

When it comes to work and finance you can now be on top form. Your practical abilities are such that you have the ability to do a dozen different things today, and keep all of them firmly on course. From a physical point of view you can tap into masses of energy and shouldn't be lacking in terms of practical common sense.

5 FRIDAY

Moon Age Day 5 Moon Sign Scorpio

The Sun still in your solar twelfth house supports a far more secretive Libra than would usually be the case. This may not even be a problem, except on those occasions when relatives or friends think you are holding out on them for some reason. At work you have scope to be extremely efficient now.

6 SATURDAY

Moon Age Day 6 Moon Sign Scorpio

There are signs that the pace of life could start to get much faster, and there may not be enough time to finish everything you want to do. Positioning yourself properly might help, as well as being willing to seek help from others. Actually some of the things you are getting anxious about are probably not at all important.

7 SUNDAY

Moon Age Day 7 Moon Sign Sagittarius

You continue to have lots of drive and energy available, funded by Mars, but at the same time that twelfth-house Sun encourages you to hold back. It's a case of two steps forward and one back, but at least that is a sort of progress. A day to keep up your efforts to sort out or even revolutionise your love life. An unexpected gift can work wonders!

8 MONDAY

Moon Age Day 8 Moon Sign Sagittarius

You might now decide you need to get away from certain people. It may not be that they infuriate you, but rather that you find them frustrating to be around. This will be especially true in the case of people who jump about from foot to foot and who refuse to actually get anything done. Your tolerance level is not high today.

9 TUESDAY

Moon Age Day 9 Moon Sign Capricorn

Venus in your solar first house assists you to ride high in a social sense and to make a significant impression when you are in public situations. That little tinge of shyness that sometimes attends the Libran nature needn't be showing now, and in most settings you should come across as being confident and capable.

10 WEDNESDAY   *Moon Age Day 10 Moon Sign Capricorn*

In addition to having the ability to get things done and feel very comfortable out there in the big wide world, you are also very much in your element when at home. The position of the Moon today encourages you to be more attentive where relations are concerned and to spend more time telling someone special how much you care about them.

11 THURSDAY   *Moon Age Day 11 Moon Sign Capricorn*

Don't expect to get all your own way in affairs of the heart today. Compromises may be needed, and some of them will be big ones. Nevertheless you need to bear in mind that the concessions you are making right now will be nothing when compared with the rewards you can achieve as a result.

12 FRIDAY   *Moon Age Day 12 Moon Sign Aquarius*

Be careful when making plans today because delays and pitfalls are possible. If you can get your head round the fact that many things will have to be organised at the last minute, you will be less frustrated in the long run. You can create some interesting social possibilities once you get work out of the way.

13 SATURDAY   *Moon Age Day 13 Moon Sign Aquarius*

There could be some very enjoyable moments around today, assisted by that first-house Venus. Social and love life offer the best opportunities at present and the weekend should offer you scope to move closer to achieving a particular desire. You might not scale the heights of pleasure but you should at least see the foothills.

14 SUNDAY   *Moon Age Day 14 Moon Sign Pisces*

Mars comes as an energy booster and now places the emphasis on physical activity, bravery and confidence. Life could be quite boisterous, and there may be a great deal of rough and tumble for young or young-at-heart Librans. Any sort of competition suits you, as would sporting activities and situations that demand stamina.

15 MONDAY *Moon Age Day 15 Moon Sign Pisces*

If you remain very active and determined you can present a picture that others find inspiring. Not everyone may be on your side though, and you need to be careful of potential rivals in some spheres of your life. Don't take it for granted that everyone who seems to be offering help is really being virtuous.

16 TUESDAY *Moon Age Day 16 Moon Sign Aries*

For the moment you would be wise to show a good deal of patience, because even if you are still champing at the bit and anxious to get things done in a big way, the lunar low does nothing to help you push forward in the way you would wish. Progress could seem slim at best, but that powerful Mars pushes you forward all the same.

17 WEDNESDAY *Moon Age Day 17 Moon Sign Aries*

The same frustrations that surfaced yesterday are still likely to be around you now. They come as a result of conflicting planetary influences. On the one side Mars urges you forward and insists that you continue to work hard towards your objectives, whilst on the other hand the Moon suggests that you take a break.

18 THURSDAY *Moon Age Day 18 Moon Sign Aries*

For the third day running you may be torn between progress and rest, though things should ease noticeably as today wears on. By this afternoon you can afford to seek support from others, and rather than responding to the more aggressive Mars, it is your Libran-placed Venus that rules you the most.

19 FRIDAY *Moon Age Day 19 Moon Sign Taurus*

You may now be far from being as sensitive to the needs of others as would normally be the case as the tug of war continues between those two adversaries, Mars and Venus. The result is that your actions can surprise certain people, particularly if you aren't yourself in specific situations. Compromise is possible, but hard to achieve.

20 SATURDAY   *Moon Age Day 20   Moon Sign Taurus*

Trends support a real yen to travel, and the arrival of the weekend could make that possible, even if you only take a short journey of some sort. You may also be in the mood to do a little shopping and there isn't much doubt that you can find some real bargains. Be prepared to stick to friends like glue in social settings.

21 SUNDAY   *Moon Age Day 21   Moon Sign Gemini*

Even little Mercury is now in your solar first house and its influence should expose you to many new and exciting ideas and possibilities. Rather than making up your mind too quickly about current projects, why not discuss situations before you reach any hard and fast conclusions? You can afford to bring new personalities into your life.

22 MONDAY   *Moon Age Day 22   Moon Sign Gemini*

Career success now comes through originality and inventiveness. You are living through very reactive and interesting times, and although life might not always be exactly easy, you can make sure it is interesting. With such a hotchpotch of planetary presence in your solar first house, just about anything is possible.

23 TUESDAY   *Moon Age Day 23   Moon Sign Cancer*

The Sun now joins Mercury, Venus and Mars in your solar first house, something that happens quite rarely and an event that offers an even more reactive and generally fortunate interlude than would usually be the case. Whether all the excitement available at the moment is strictly to your liking remains to be seen. You can easily get tired.

24 WEDNESDAY   *Moon Age Day 24   Moon Sign Cancer*

The accent now is on close, personal attachments. The time is right to work towards companionship in everything you do, so you may not be too content when you have to soldier on alone. Doing things in pairs and in groups is favoured under present trends and you can certainly be the life and soul of any party.

25 THURSDAY ☿ *Moon Age Day 25 Moon Sign Leo*

There are warm friendships to be made and new attachments to be formed all the time under present trends. Potentially active and very enterprising, you can move towards your overall objectives in a very positive way and won't be easily swayed once you have made up your mind. It's worth dismissing the usual hesitance of Libra for now.

26 FRIDAY ☿ *Moon Age Day 26 Moon Sign Leo*

Communications are well accented, assisting you to relish the company of people who have something interesting to say. Your nature is cultured and refined – to the extent that you may well feel quite uncomfortable with people you see as lacking in social graces. You can get most people to respond to your nature now.

27 SATURDAY ☿ *Moon Age Day 27 Moon Sign Virgo*

There may be something of the warrior about you at the moment and this is thanks to the present position of Mars, which simmers away in your solar first house and encourages you to be braver and even more foolhardy than usual. If ever you wished to do something completely out of the ordinary, this is the time to do it!

28 SUNDAY ☿ *Moon Age Day 28 Moon Sign Virgo*

It's time to capitalise on all sorts of opportunities that you wouldn't even notice as a rule. Trends support your great verve and a strong desire to stretch the possible into the incredible. Whether or not you actually succeed is in some doubt, but in a sense it doesn't really matter. It's putting in the effort that really counts.

29 MONDAY ☿ *Moon Age Day 29 Moon Sign Libra*

You have what it takes to look and feel at your best. This is the most fortunate time of a very positive period and the lunar high this month is worth a great deal in terms of potential successes. Don't take no for an answer, and if you have made up your mind to any particular course of action you need to stick to it like glue.

30 TUESDAY ☿ *Moon Age Day 0 Moon Sign Libra*

A physical and mental peak is possible, and you can continue to be very positive in your attitude. Libra is rarely this certain of itself and you have scope to make great progress in almost anything you undertake now. You show great powers of concentration and an in-built desire to make everyone happy.

October

2008

1 WEDNESDAY ☿ *Moon Age Day 1 Moon Sign Libra*

This has to be a great start to a new month. In addition to the lunar high, Venus has now moved into your solar second house and from this position it can be very useful in terms of your money-making abilities. The only slight problem is that in addition to attracting cash at the moment you may also be tempted to spend it quite quickly.

2 THURSDAY ☿ *Moon Age Day 2 Moon Sign Scorpio*

Trends encourage optimism regarding a new project, and even if it is early days you can make sure things work out well for you. This optimism is not misplaced and you are also in a good position to attract the positive help of people who are really in the know. All in all you should be poised to make real progress.

3 FRIDAY ☿ *Moon Age Day 3 Moon Sign Scorpio*

You remain mentally alert and have the ability to think quickly and to act almost instantly. This potentially progressive phase has been so long that you might be running out of steam, but whenever you feel tired, you can find something newer and more interesting. You could surprise yourself with the level of your stamina.

4 SATURDAY ☿ *Moon Age Day 4 Moon Sign Sagittarius*

It is clearly the right time to take centre-stage, especially in social settings. You can ensure that there is nothing remotely routine about your life at the moment, and you can revel in good company and exciting times. If nothing seems to be happening, why not turn up the power of your mind and grab something from the ether? It's good to be Libran now.

5 SUNDAY ☿ *Moon Age Day 5 Moon Sign Sagittarius*

There may not be time to do everything you planned today and it would be quite sensible to decide early what is most important to you and to concentrate on that. If there are arguments within the family you would be well advised to stay away from them and may decide to spend the majority of your day with friends.

6 MONDAY ☿ *Moon Age Day 6 Moon Sign Sagittarius*

The focus is on family life at the moment, and you may not be contributing quite as much as usual out there in the wider world. Real fulfilment presently lies amongst your nearest and dearest but this is likely to be a temporary interlude since outside events could demand you much more by tomorrow.

7 TUESDAY ☿ *Moon Age Day 7 Moon Sign Capricorn*

Fluctuating finances are a distinct possibility at the moment, and a degree of care would be sensible. Listen to the wise advice of an older family member or friend when it comes to some sort of deal that looks rather too good to be true. Your own instincts are really all you need.

8 WEDNESDAY ☿ *Moon Age Day 8 Moon Sign Capricorn*

The focus is still predominantly on finance, and present trends are more favourable. There is unlikely to be a fortune coming your way right today, but little by little there are gains to be made. Strategies made in order to gain more through your work tend to be sound now.

9 THURSDAY ☿ *Moon Age Day 9 Moon Sign Aquarius*

Life now means enjoyment and you have what it takes to have a good time. You also have scope to be extremely creative at the moment, and although there is nothing remotely odd about that, you can turn your creativity into cash if you think for a while about skills you already possess.

10 FRIDAY ☿ *Moon Age Day 10 Moon Sign Aquarius*

This is a high ego point for Libra and a time during which you can positively demand the attention of the world at large. It might be sensible to start with friends and colleagues, few of whom should fail to notice your attractive nature at the moment. You might not feel much like working hard today, but you will probably know how to party!

11 SATURDAY ☿ *Moon Age Day 11 Moon Sign Aquarius*

A potentially lucrative period continues and financial progress may be possible in surprising directions. A strong desire for luxury is also indicated, and you may choose to be in surroundings that are comfortable and pleasing to the eye. Little passes your attention today, either at work or home.

12 SUNDAY ☿ *Moon Age Day 12 Moon Sign Pisces*

As long as you keep things organised you can ensure there are no setbacks today. Much depends on your ability to keep a sense of proportion regarding issues that really don't need you to get involved. The problem is that a slightly nosey streak is crossing the Libran path today, and you just can't avoid interfering!

13 MONDAY ☿ *Moon Age Day 13 Moon Sign Pisces*

You are still inclined to rush in where angels fear to tread. If that means you are doing something that annoys family members, you may be in for a roasting as a result. Bearing in mind how much you hate any sort of fuss or argument, it might still be better to let people do what they want, even if you know they are misguided.

14 TUESDAY ☿ *Moon Age Day 14 Moon Sign Aries*

A day to put major issues on the back burner whilst you take a break and simply relax. This may not be easy under all circumstances, because although the lunar low suggests that you tire quickly, it also encourages worrying over issues that would, under normal circumstances, be left to sort themselves out.

15 WEDNESDAY ☿   *Moon Age Day 15   Moon Sign Aries*

Now you really do need to take life one step at a time because if you rush things there's a chance you will go wrong. Your thinking processes could be slightly clouded – maybe by sentiment – and you need more time to do practically everything. It's worth seeking out a little help, particularly if there are people around who are just bursting to lend a hand.

16 THURSDAY ☿   *Moon Age Day 16 Moon Sign Taurus*

The lunar low is out of the way and you can now do much towards broadening your personal horizons. This is especially true when it comes to intellectual and cultural interests. All in all it would be good to keep up a fairly high social profile and to let everyone know that you are in the market for new forms of stimulation.

17 FRIDAY   *Moon Age Day 17 Moon Sign Taurus*

You can now capitalise on business and financial investments and make the most of unexpected assistance in your efforts to increase your salary. Gifts are also possible – though one or two of these might be difficult to recognise as such in the beginning. A sideways look at life perhaps works best for Libra today.

18 SATURDAY   *Moon Age Day 18 Moon Sign Gemini*

Continue to look out for new chances and opportunities that are on offer at this time. If you need financial assistance in order to develop your ideas, you have scope to think up unique ways to get it. On the way you need to guard against waste or extravagance, because you hate both and wouldn't be happy with yourself if you failed to do so.

19 SUNDAY   *Moon Age Day 19 Moon Sign Gemini*

The planetary line-up will certainly allow you to get where you want to be today, with only a little ingenious assistance on your part. You needn't let anything stand in the way of your aims and wishes, though your constant tendency to doubt yourself doesn't always help. What you need to use right now is undeniable confidence.

20 MONDAY
Moon Age Day 20 Moon Sign Cancer

The Moon in your solar tenth house continues to offer assistance in financial matters, but does little to make the domestic path as smooth as you would wish. If what is happening there is beyond your abilities to control, why not spend at least some of your spare time today with friends?

21 TUESDAY
Moon Age Day 21 Moon Sign Cancer

Trends support a great drive towards financial gain and a heightened desire to increase your sense of personal security. Although Libra is likely to act on impulse under most circumstances and at many times, this facet of your nature is far less enhanced under present planetary trends. Most of your moves should now be sound.

22 WEDNESDAY
Moon Age Day 22 Moon Sign Leo

This is an excellent time to be out there making new friends – some of whom have what it takes to enhance your social position and standing. These things are important to Libra, who doesn't like to slum it very much. You prefer sensitive and genteel types right now and might positively shun any sort of vulgarity or dodgy-dealing.

23 THURSDAY
Moon Age Day 23 Moon Sign Leo

Everyday life offers you scope to keep on the go and you needn't be at all reticent to push your luck a little when you can see the path ahead clearly. If friends have a special need of you at present, be prepared to give advice and practical assistance. Putting yourself out for others should be no hardship.

24 FRIDAY
Moon Age Day 24 Moon Sign Virgo

This has potential to be a time of financial strength. The Sun has now moved into your solar second house and this solidifies your ability to make things work the way you would wish. You might not be quite as capricious as was the case earlier in the month, but to compensate your money-management skills are well starred.

25 SATURDAY   *Moon Age Day 25 Moon Sign Virgo*

Don't take things to heart at a personal level, particularly if there are remarks being made at the moment that are not directed at you, but to which you might attach yourself. Getting hold of the wrong end of the stick is all too easy under present trends, but before you show a strong reaction to anything you ought to think very carefully.

26 SUNDAY   *Moon Age Day 26 Moon Sign Virgo*

A slightly quieter day might be not only possible but highly desirable right now. By tomorrow you can get right back in gear and can do whatever it takes to make significant progress, but this is probably not the case for now. Don't be afraid to let others help you out – or better still allow them to do more or less everything for the moment.

27 MONDAY   *Moon Age Day 27 Moon Sign Libra*

Along comes another high-energy period and a time in which you should be firing on all cylinders. You know all too well what you want from life and will have some really good ideas when it comes to getting it. Not everyone seems to be on your side, but with the lunar high around you probably needn't worry too much about dissenters.

28 TUESDAY   *Moon Age Day 28 Moon Sign Libra*

This is the best time of all to put new ideas and strategies to the test. Now less hesitant than you have been for the last couple of weeks you can throw caution to the wind and act with much greater force. Desires are emphasised, and this also feeds the romantic side of your nature, making it possible to sweep someone completely off their feet.

29 WEDNESDAY   *Moon Age Day 0 Moon Sign Scorpio*

Opportunities for progress continue unabated, even if you don't have quite the dynamism of the last couple of days. You may decide to tone down your powers just a little but can be every bit as effective – and possibly more so. Libra has scope to exude confidence that is easily picked up by others, most of whom respond positively.

30 THURSDAY   *Moon Age Day 1 Moon Sign Scorpio*

The focus is on your sensitivity to your working and living environment and to the natures of other people. Back your hunches all the way because your intuition is as strong as it gets. When it comes to talks or negotiations you can work wonders, and will be so tuned-in that you can handle several different situations at the same time.

31 FRIDAY   *Moon Age Day 2 Moon Sign Sagittarius*

You look and feel strong when going after your objectives, but there is just a slight tendency that you could become slightly too confident for your own good. If you still need help in some spheres of life be prepared to seek extra support, partcularly regarding any issue that could be best described as 'specialised'.

November
2008

1 SATURDAY
Moon Age Day 3 Moon Sign Sagittarius

With the Sun strong in your solar second house the emphasis remains on resourcefulness and on control of your personal resources. You can afford to devote your energy to investments and towards making money, though at the same time it is clear that a change of scene could work wonders this weekend.

2 SUNDAY
Moon Age Day 4 Moon Sign Sagittarius

There could be some slight setbacks today, but if you register these at all you will also have what it takes to address them successfully. If relationships with family and friends are difficult, why not simply concentrate on romance, which is definitely favoured now?

3 MONDAY
Moon Age Day 5 Moon Sign Capricorn

Trends enhance your memory at the moment, so you can use it to the full, especially at work or in matters of education. You can surprise others with your powers of recall and can turn this phase very much to your advantage. From a social point of view you can now get on well with some fairly unusual types.

4 TUESDAY
Moon Age Day 6 Moon Sign Capricorn

You have what it takes to use your considerable charm to get your own way in most situations. You will enjoy being amongst all types of people and needn't be nervous, even if you are the centre of attention. On the contrary, you become the consummate actor under present planetary trends.

5 WEDNESDAY   *Moon Age Day 7 Moon Sign Aquarius*

There is still a strong emphasis on the fun side of life. Your charm helps you to attract new admirers and Libran people who are not involved in a romantic attachment at present could well find new love around this time. For those who are settled, today offers a chance for a special kind of happiness.

6 THURSDAY   *Moon Age Day 8 Moon Sign Aquarius*

It looks as though your powers of concentration are especially well accented at the moment, and you seem to be able to hold a great deal in your head. It is possible that colleagues and friends have great need of your special abilities, and you can afford to give a good deal of your time today to supporting those around you.

7 FRIDAY   *Moon Age Day 9 Moon Sign Aquarius*

Your strength now lies in being useful, which is why you might be doing all you can to be of assistance to practically everyone you meet. In particular you could enjoy improving things, and this is likely to be the case both at work and at home. Librans who have been slightly off colour recently should now be feeling better.

8 SATURDAY   *Moon Age Day 10 Moon Sign Pisces*

Your efforts generally continue to find practical applications, but you do need to be slightly more careful at the moment when it comes to money. On the one hand you could be spending more than you can afford, but on the other you don't want to miss what is definitely a great bargain. It's a case of treading a fine line.

9 SUNDAY   *Moon Age Day 11 Moon Sign Pisces*

The focus is still on money, and the trends today are slightly better. Be prepared to firm up on financial securities and plan well ahead. In a more personal sense there are romantic interludes today and a definite need to be somewhere other than your usual Sunday haunts.

143

10 MONDAY　　　　　*Moon Age Day 12　Moon Sign Aries*

The lunar low could now encourage you to worry too much about details today and tomorrow. As long as you realise what is happening, and why, this need not be any sort of problem. At the same time you could feel thwarted if something you really want doesn't seem to be working out as you had hoped.

11 TUESDAY　　　　　*Moon Age Day 13　Moon Sign Aries*

There are a few limitations about, and even if the lunar low is not especially potent this time around you do need to be on your guard. Bear in mind that there may be people around who are not at all what they appear to be on the surface. Turn your intuition up to full power and listen carefully to that little voice within your head.

12 WEDNESDAY　　　　*Moon Age Day 14　Moon Sign Taurus*

With the lunar low now out of the way it is the little planet Mercury that seems to be influencing you more than any other influence. The financial trends should be better and your tendency to seek out new goals and little adventures is likely to be strong. In terms of your work there could be a definite easing of pressure today.

13 THURSDAY　　　　*Moon Age Day 15　Moon Sign Taurus*

Domestic and intimate matters are to the fore, and probably in a very positive way. The time is right to confide any small problems to loved ones, whilst at the same time acting as a sounding board if others are feeling pressured. In all your associations with other people you can be kind, attentive and filled with ideas.

14 FRIDAY　　　　　*Moon Age Day 16　Moon Sign Gemini*

You can now make the very best of opportunities that come your way, and this is especially noticeable at work. Whatever the recent state of affairs has been for you, you now have what it takes to improve things quite significantly. If routines are a bit of a chore at the moment, it's worth looking for something new.

15 SATURDAY   *Moon Age Day 17 Moon Sign Gemini*

The Moon in your solar fifth house is all about widening your mental horizons and actively seeking out other people who are on the same mental wavelength. Don't be afraid to mix with unusual sorts of people at the moment. No matter what sort of individuals they may be, you can gain something from them.

16 SUNDAY   *Moon Age Day 18 Moon Sign Cancer*

Today offers scope to enjoy a peaceful home and family life, which under present planetary trends will be most welcome. This would be an ideal time to beautify your surroundings, and to that end you could be getting out the paint and the wallpaper. Remember not to make too much mess because that is what you hate most!

17 MONDAY   *Moon Age Day 19 Moon Sign Cancer*

Both home and career offer rewards this week, and there might be moments when you are torn between them. A journey into the past could be fairly rewarding and might cheer you up, but it is important to remember that what really matters is in the present and the future. Libra can sometimes be a little too dreamy for its own good.

18 TUESDAY   *Moon Age Day 20 Moon Sign Leo*

Today the planet Mars enters your solar third house and this could have a definite bearing on your life over the next few weeks. You need to be quite careful to ensure that whatever you say to others is fully understood – and also that you know exactly what you are trying to put across. If you are vague, difficulties could follow.

19 WEDNESDAY   *Moon Age Day 21 Moon Sign Leo*

Right now you have a natural ability to organise group activities. It doesn't really matter whether this is at home, at work, or for social settings. If you remain confident, you can persuade others to follow your lead, and getting anyone to do anything is now merely a case of turning up your charm to its 'full' setting.

20 THURSDAY
Moon Age Day 22 Moon Sign Leo

With the Moon now moving into your solar twelfth house later today, a little confusion is possible, together with a quieter time than of late. Don't be too quick to take on new responsibilities, and where possible you may decide to defer to someone who definitely has more experience than you do.

21 FRIDAY
Moon Age Day 23 Moon Sign Virgo

Family relationships could be the dominant factor in your thinking, and you may well spend a good deal of your time today trying to get others to agree. Getting involved in heated discussions would not be wise today. Your best option is to seek a little seclusion if you think that things are getting out of hand.

22 SATURDAY
Moon Age Day 24 Moon Sign Virgo

You can make this a weekend of two halves. Today offers a quiet interlude, with a chance to spend time on your own, but this is a trend that should soon disappear towards the end of the day. By the evening you can afford to contemplate having fun, and by the end of the night you should be creating it!

23 SUNDAY
Moon Age Day 25 Moon Sign Libra

Right now you should find both personal and professional aims and objectives very easy to address. If you work at the weekend today could be especially rewarding, and it looks as though a personal coup is possible at any moment. On the other hand if your time is your own today, it's worth finding new ways to have some fun.

24 MONDAY
Moon Age Day 26 Moon Sign Libra

Trends are still favourable, and if either business or personal initiatives are well overdue, this is the time to chase them for all you are worth. Finances are well starred, in terms of both the deals you can make and the money you can obtain.

25 TUESDAY   *Moon Age Day 27 Moon Sign Scorpio*

This has potential to be a hardworking period and a time when you can concentrate almost exclusively on feathering your nest for the future. Your powers of recall might be especially good, and you can enjoy the cut and thrust of relationships old and new. The horizons look positive, and thinking about the future is right up your street.

26 WEDNESDAY   *Moon Age Day 28 Moon Sign Scorpio*

The emphasis is definitely on communication now and this is thanks to the position of the Sun, which presently occupies your solar third house. There is likely to be a bit of battle going on here because Mars is also in this part of your solar chart. As a result, today could be a balancing act between amenable and feisty!

27 THURSDAY   *Moon Age Day 29 Moon Sign Scorpio*

You can use what you hear from others today to enhance your overall feelings of happiness and your sense that most situations are going the way you would wish. In the main you know where your life is going and might be quite content to let certain matters take their own course. Relaxation would be no bad thing.

28 FRIDAY   *Moon Age Day 0 Moon Sign Sagittarius*

There are signs that you may be putting across your ideas too dynamically for others to cope with. Libra is, after all, an Air sign and can be quite enthusiastic about almost anything. Quieter types might find your attitude too strident or definite and a slight alteration in technique may help. However, in the end you have to follow your own path.

29 SATURDAY   *Moon Age Day 1 Moon Sign Sagittarius*

Trends suggest that you are presently trying to achieve too much and it would do you a great deal of good to use this weekend as a way of looking at matters again, this time with a good deal more self-criticism than you have been employing of late. You needn't let this process get in the way of having fun, because there are good times to be had.

30 SUNDAY   *Moon Age Day 2 Moon Sign Capricorn*

Once again it is communication that can be your salvation. Use your third-house Sun because it allows you to explain yourself more fully and to get your message across to people who can sometimes be difficult. Family members could be a source of joy and you may decide to spend time with them today.

December
2008

1 MONDAY
Moon Age Day 3 Moon Sign Capricorn

Venus is now in your solar fourth house and from that position it brings a new and fulfilling trend affecting the domestic landscape. This will be your main sphere of influence and fulfilment across the next few days at least. Younger family members in particular could give you pause for thought and new ideas.

2 TUESDAY
Moon Age Day 4 Moon Sign Capricorn

This is a day when you can be the life and soul of the party – that is if there is one happening today. There is a strong boost to your romantic potential and a desire to be out there enjoying yourself. It looks as though you can make the Christmas spirit come early this year – at least as far as the sign of Libra is concerned.

3 WEDNESDAY
Moon Age Day 5 Moon Sign Aquarius

Your strength now lies in your progressive and logical thinking, which is more than can be said for some of your friends and colleagues. Not everyone is equally sensible in their appraisal of situations today – which is why it's worth being much more discriminating yourself, even if that makes you unpopular.

4 THURSDAY
Moon Age Day 6 Moon Sign Aquarius

You now enter a period of hard work, even though in some situations you may be putting in more effort than is strictly necessary. At least by doing things the hard way you can be certain that they are done properly, and that is what seems to matter the most to you now. Routines should prove to be comfortable rather than irritating at present.

5 FRIDAY
Moon Age Day 7   Moon Sign Pisces

You can make this a fairly fulfilling period in terms of domestic matters, particularly if family members are both compliant and charming right now. Could they have their eyes on potential Christmas gifts? It's possible, but too much cynicism is to be avoided under present planetary trends. Just accept their more reasonable attitude.

6 SATURDAY
Moon Age Day 8   Moon Sign Pisces

Travel and conversations are positively highlighted today, assisting you to mix quite freely with all manner of people on your journey through Saturday. This would be a good time for shopping, though probably not on your own. Friends are great to have around when there are bargains to be sought, and you can have a chat too!

7 SUNDAY
Moon Age Day 9   Moon Sign Pisces

A quieter day is possible, though by no means inevitable right now. Even if some of your earlier cheerfulness is rubbing off on those around you, from a personal point of view you may not be quite so effervescent as would often be the case. Maybe you have things on your mind but it's more likely you are spending time planning ahead.

8 MONDAY
Moon Age Day 10   Moon Sign Aries

If it seems as if everyone else is getting ahead much better and faster than you are, it is the lunar low that should take the blame. Actually it may not be too potent this time around, and it does at least give you the chance to move away from the social spotlight and think about all those jobs that are still to be done but which you haven't addressed yet.

9 TUESDAY
Moon Age Day 11   Moon Sign Aries

To compensate for the Moon being in Aries, you do have that third-house Mars, which supports a noisier Libra than would normally be the case whilst the lunar low is around. You can also show yourself to be quite alert and discriminating, though it might be better not to make too many long-term decisions until tomorrow.

10 WEDNESDAY   *Moon Age Day 12 Moon Sign Taurus*

Trends encourage mental effort and an insatiable curiosity about a thousand different things. Keep up with correspondence and don't forget all those Christmas cards you probably haven't even purchased yet. It's a busy life, and you may have to compartmentalise the day in order to get everything done.

11 THURSDAY   *Moon Age Day 13 Moon Sign Taurus*

Now you can really benefit from having many different sorts of people around you. You have what it takes to show the most gregarious and humorous side of your nature throughout today, and this is an ideal time for socialising ahead of the Christmas period itself. You always seem to know exactly what to say.

12 FRIDAY   *Moon Age Day 14 Moon Sign Gemini*

You have scope to show a strongly independent streak and to use this to widen your horizons. Closer to the end of the month you might find any real progress difficult to make, not because of planetary influences but on account of Christmas. That's why it is so important to push ahead at the moment and make a real display of your talents.

13 SATURDAY   *Moon Age Day 15 Moon Sign Gemini*

Even if you are quick-witted at the moment, you might also be quite egocentric in some ways – which can be the cause of disputes with certain other people. On odd rare occasions it will be a case of an irresistible force meeting an irremovable object, but since Libra is ever the diplomat, you can afford to be the one to back down.

14 SUNDAY   *Moon Age Day 16 Moon Sign Cancer*

This may be one of the best days of the month to initiate new projects and to get life moving at a fairly heady pace. Now is the time to seek assistance from people who have real influence. People from the past could well be coming into your mind, but that is normal for December.

15 MONDAY
Moon Age Day 17   Moon Sign Cancer

Venus has now moved on into your solar fifth house – racing ahead as it sometimes appears to do when viewed from the Earth. This influence supports an easy-going time socially and the ability to display your love of life on most occasions. If there are any frustrations these could well come about because of family behaviour.

16 TUESDAY
Moon Age Day 18   Moon Sign Leo

Friendships continue to be a source of reward in your life at the moment and today could see newcomers on the horizon. Maybe you will meet these people because of Christmas social obligations or it could be that you will come across them in the course of your working life. Wherever they appear, trends suggest you should take notice.

17 WEDNESDAY
Moon Age Day 19   Moon Sign Leo

Mental organisation and efficiency may not be all they should be right now, and with the Moon approaching your solar twelfth house you could more easily become confused by issues that normally give you no trouble at all. On the positive side of the coin you are in a position to use your charm to break down any sort of social barrier.

18 THURSDAY
Moon Age Day 20   Moon Sign Virgo

Your affable Libran charm makes everyone around you keen to know you better and your popularity can be as high as generally proves to be the case. Whether you are satisfied with your own efforts at the moment remains to be seen. In some ways this could be one of those 'red light days' during which little things constantly delay you.

19 FRIDAY
Moon Age Day 21   Moon Sign Virgo

Even if you are still a little quieter than would usually be the case, as today advances you should have less interruptions and a greater ability to get what you want from life in a general sense. Getting things done more quickly, you need to be careful to ensure that details are sorted out properly before you move on to new jobs.

20 SATURDAY *Moon Age Day 22 Moon Sign Libra*

Mental and physical strengths are evident and for the next two days you are able to achieve a great deal that you failed to address earlier in the month. Make the most of the energy you have available and the enthusiasm that is a natural consequence of being a Libran. Don't analyse these trends – simply use them.

21 SUNDAY *Moon Age Day 23 Moon Sign Libra*

Where important objectives are concerned you should not be afraid to take the odd chance. That doesn't mean putting yourself in any sort of danger, but rather striking whilst the iron is hot when it comes to controlling your own life. From a financial point of view you have scope for some progress now.

22 MONDAY *Moon Age Day 24 Moon Sign Scorpio*

You need to be both socially and romantically active today if you want to get the very best out of what present trends are offering. There is no point at all in sitting in a corner and waiting for life to come to you. On the contrary, you should promote good times rather than reacting to them. If you have plenty of ideas in your head, it should be easy!

23 TUESDAY *Moon Age Day 25 Moon Sign Scorpio*

A day to take the credit for some very bold ideas, particularly if you are quite adventurous right now. Most of what you undertake now is for purely social reasons and to extend your goodwill at Christmas, but there are still a few positive and practical steps you can take in order to better your lot in life for later.

24 WEDNESDAY *Moon Age Day 26 Moon Sign Scorpio*

A new idea or pursuit could prove to be quite inspiring today, though you may not have too much time to think about it. It is towards the enjoyment of others that your mind tends to turn on Christmas Eve, and you can get a great deal of enjoyment yourself from your efforts to make the whole world smile.

25 THURSDAY   *Moon Age Day 27 Moon Sign Sagittarius*

Christmas Day has potential to be both happy and significant this year. With almost all details sorted out you should be able to sit back and enjoy yourself at least a little. Of course there are always things to be done, and maybe not everyone is pulling their weight as they should. The odd little nudge may be necessary.

26 FRIDAY   *Moon Age Day 28 Moon Sign Sagittarius*

It is time for a stimulating love life, and Boxing Day offers the best chance of romance across the entire Christmas period. Perhaps this is because you have more hours to concentrate on such matters, or simply because you are in the right place at the best possible time. Friendships can also be strengthened under present planetary trends.

27 SATURDAY   *Moon Age Day 0 Moon Sign Capricorn*

Mars is still in your solar third house, offering sharper mental processes, even if it can also make you slightly more reactive on occasions. Be prepared to welcome people you don't see all that often to your life at the moment. They could bring with them a great deal of Christmas nostalgia.

28 SUNDAY   *Moon Age Day 1 Moon Sign Capricorn*

You could be rather too emotional for your own good at present and it would be better not to allow yourself to wallow in the past more than is strictly necessary. Get out one of those games you got for Christmas or else travel a short distance to somewhere that you find particularly interesting. This is not a good day to spend too much time alone.

29 MONDAY   *Moon Age Day 2 Moon Sign Capricorn*

The Moon now favours your domestic circumstances, which might mean you don't have to do all the tidying up yourself or that relatives are just being kinder than is sometimes the case. Peace and quiet at home is more than simply pleasant at the moment, and is something you long for after all the activity and socialising.

30 TUESDAY *Moon Age Day 3 Moon Sign Aquarius*

A successful time is achievable on most fronts, though you may not be able to get things moving quite as quickly as you might wish. Trends encourage you to take a far more dynamic role in romantic matters and to be extremely creative at the moment. Changes in and around your home are quite possible.

31 WEDNESDAY *Moon Age Day 4 Moon Sign Aquarius*

Affairs of the heart continue to be positively highlighted as the year draws to its close. You can put yourself in the best of company today and so the possibilities for a good New Year party are in place. This is an especially good time for twosomes and for romantic liaisons – even on occasion if you haven't been expecting them.

RISING SIGNS FOR LIBRA

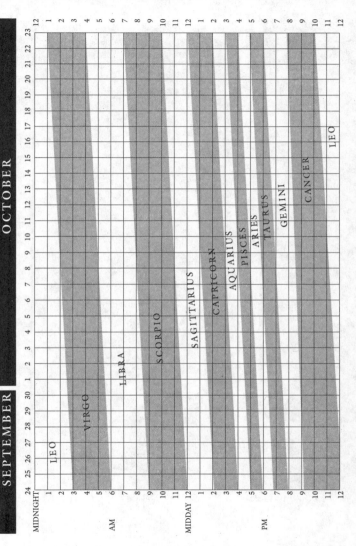

THE ZODIAC, PLANETS
AND CORRESPONDENCES

The Earth revolves around the Sun once every calendar year, so when viewed from Earth the Sun appears in a different part of the sky as the year progresses. In astrology, these parts of the sky are divided into the signs of the zodiac and this means that the signs are organised in a circle. The circle begins with Aries and ends with Pisces.

Taking the zodiac sign as a starting point, astrologers then work with all the positions of planets, stars and many other factors to calculate horoscopes and birth charts and tell us what the stars have in store for us.

The table below shows the planets and Elements for each of the signs of the zodiac. Each sign belongs to one of the four Elements: Fire, Air, Earth or Water. Fire signs are creative and enthusiastic; Air signs are mentally active and thoughtful; Earth signs are constructive and practical; Water signs are emotional and have strong feelings.

It also shows the metals and gemstones associated with, or corresponding with, each sign. The correspondence is made when a metal or stone possesses properties that are held in common with a particular sign of the zodiac.

Finally, the table shows the opposite of each star sign – this is the opposite sign in the astrological circle.

Placed	Sign	Symbol	Element	Planet	Metal	Stone	Opposite
1	Aries	Ram	Fire	Mars	Iron	Bloodstone	Libra
2	Taurus	Bull	Earth	Venus	Copper	Sapphire	Scorpio
3	Gemini	Twins	Air	Mercury	Mercury	Tiger's Eye	Sagittarius
4	Cancer	Crab	Water	Moon	Silver	Pearl	Capricorn
5	Leo	Lion	Fire	Sun	Gold	Ruby	Aquarius
6	Virgo	Maiden	Earth	Mercury	Mercury	Sardonyx	Pisces
7	Libra	Scales	Air	Venus	Copper	Sapphire	Aries
8	Scorpio	Scorpion	Water	Pluto	Plutonium	Jasper	Taurus
9	Sagittarius	Archer	Fire	Jupiter	Tin	Topaz	Gemini
10	Capricorn	Goat	Earth	Saturn	Lead	Black Onyx	Cancer
11	Aquarius	Waterbearer	Air	Uranus	Uranium	Amethyst	Leo
12	Pisces	Fishes	Water	Neptune	Tin	Moonstone	Virgo